You Can Raise
Courageous &
Confident Kids

Mary E. DeMuth

HARVEST HOUSE PUBLISHERS

EUGENE, OREGON

Published in association with the literary agency of Alive Communications, Inc., 7680 Goddard Street, Ste #200, Colorado Springs, CO 80920. *www.alivecommunications.com.*

Cover photo © iStockphoto / monkeybusiness images

Cover by Left Coast Design, Portland, Oregon

YOU CAN RAISE COURAGEOUS AND CONFIDENT KIDS
Copyright © 2007 by Mary DeMuth
Published by Harvest House Publishers
Eugene, Oregon 97402
www.harvesthousepublishers.com

Library of Congress Cataloging-in-Publication Data
DeMuth, Mary E.
   [Authentic parenting in a postmodern culture]
   You can raise courageous and confident kids / Mary E. DeMuth.
     p. cm.
   Originally published: Authentic parenting in a postmodern culture. ©2007. With additional material added.
   Includes bibliographical references (p.   ).
   ISBN 978-0-7369-2971-4 (pbk.)
   1. Parenting—Religious aspects—Christianity. I. Title.
   BV4529.D46 2011
   248.8'45—dc22

                                        2010028944

inner world as *modern*, and I did not dare call my new thoughts *postmodern* for fear of being seen as evil, I knew my thinking had shifted radically. As our church-planting organization educated us about the cultural shift that is postmodernism, Patrick and I nodded a lot. We resonated with what was said. Eventually, we moved our family thousands of miles away to the hotbed of postmodernity—Western Europe.

Our sojourn there was the context in which I wrote this book—initially to help parents navigate the world outside their front doors. Its original title was *Authentic Parenting in a Postmodern Culture*. My goal was to empower parents to help their children flourish spiritually regardless of what the culture dictated.

Now that my eldest child is kissing adulthood, I am vitally interested in how my children have learned to love others and live out the gospel of Jesus Christ courageously and confidently. As I prepared them to meet the culture, I realized that in doing so, something shifted all of us. The more we elevated Jesus, the more we fell in love with Him and His radical ways as a family, the more my kids exuded Christ's courage. My eldest daughter, Sophie, led her friend to Jesus. My son, Aidan, stood up to bullies. My youngest daughter, Julia, endured a difficult teacher. All with courage and all with confidence. Hence the retitling of this book.

In these pages, I grapple with a question you may have wondered or worried about: What is a biblical, timeless view of parenting?

I write this to reassure you. Like you, I am a learner. I don't have all the answers. But I do have a highly unusual testing ground of experience. Our family lived in a culture hostile to Christianity, and by the grace of God, my children thrived. We now live on American soil after two and a half years overseas. We faced many trials on a global scale, but we endured them together. My children are courageous—so much so that they challenge me to take more risks and trust Jesus for more. They're confident—in their faith, in our family, and, ultimately, in themselves.

What's a Parent to Do?

Regardless of the cultural situation in which we find ourselves, we parents are still called on to love our children with sacrificial love. We

A Caveat

The first time I heard about a cultural shift, I was a young mother, saturated in the throes of diapers, toddler tantrums, and primordial exhaustion. I brushed the notion aside, thinking it unimportant—completely unrelated to my life as a mother. The next time I heard about it was in the context of evil. Radio voices warned about the slippery slope of postmodern thinking and the inherent wrongness of a new worldview. Again, this seemed detached from my very real life as a preschool parent, the day-to-day joy and grind of raising the next generation (while I cleaned peanut butter from every surface). Although I largely ignored the alarming statements, a bit of fear infused itself into my heart. Not really knowing what postmodernism was, I envisioned it a malevolent force, like the New Age proliferation of the '80s.

The next time I heard whispers about cultural shift, my children were all three walking and talking and making their own peanut butter and jelly sandwiches—no more diapers, still some tantrums. My husband, Patrick, and I were exploring church planting in Western Europe, and the terms *postmodern* and *emergent* circulated around us.

A Shift

Something shifted in me in that interim period between ignoring and fearing a cultural shift. I started thinking in new ways. I became dissatisfied with parts of my Christian subculture, but I couldn't put that underlying unease into words. Although I could not pigeonhole my past

Contents

Acknowledgments

Patrick, I couldn't have written this book without you. Thank you for listening to my constant postmodern ramblings, for offering advice when I needed it, and for believing this book must be written. I love you.

This book is better because of my critique group, Life Sentence. Leslie and D'Ann, I needed your extra set of eyes as well as your unique experiences as parents.

A hearty thanks goes to my prayer team, who sacrificed time to pray alongside me: Kevin and Renee Bailey, Colleen Eslinger, Sandi Glahn, Jack and Helen Graves, Kim Griffith, Ed and Sue Harrell, Debbie Hutchison, Katy Raymond, Hud and Nancy McWilliams, Michael and Renee Mills, Kim Moore, Marilyn Neel, Caroline O'Neill, Kathy O'Neill, Don Pape, Catalin and Shannon Popa, Tom and Holly Schmidt, Carla Smith, Erin Teske, Jim and Stacey Tomisser, Janet Turner, JR and Ginger Vassar, Rod and Mary Vestal, Jodie Westfall, Denise Wilhite, Betsy Williams, Jan Winebrenner, and Liz Wolf. As this book blesses parents and gives them a voice, I applaud your prayers.

Brandy Prince, thank you for that wonderful conversation via Skype about coaching and parenting. I still think you need to write that book!

A hearty thank you for those who were interviewed for the book: Will and Lisa Samson, Steve and Erin Teske, Byron and Lisa Borden, Michael and Renee Mills, Phil and Laina Graf, Troy and Heather Cady, JR and Ginger Vassar, George and Jeanne Damoff, and Justin and Jen Powell.

Sophie, Aidan, and Julia, it seems strange, doesn't it, that your mommy had to spend time away from you while she wrote about parenting. I am so thankful, though, that you are children of grace, that you love me in the midst of deadlines. My hat goes off to you, and my heart as well.

Jesus, it's all about You.

To Darci, Jim, Taylor, and Micah Rubart:
a courageous and confident family

must be models of grace. We are responsible to train our children. Cultural shift does not release us from the responsibility of providing good spiritual foundations in our home. But our changing times radically affect the manner in which we parent. To prepare our children to engage in their world, we must embrace dialogue, community, the world. We must reorient ourselves beyond the four walls of our insulated homes. We must see our parenting as a kindred journey with our children, a coming alongside.

In that journey, I am a newcomer. Like you, I am learning. I still make many, many mistakes. So that's my caveat. I'm writing this book for my sake as well as yours—to learn the value of exegeting both culture and the Bible and to do so with a heart of humility.

You won't find the ten steps to perfect parenting within these pages. Nor will you find a random approach to parenting. I hope what I offer here is life—the life of Jesus infused into our imperfect homes in this shifting, imperfect world. Because ultimately His life gives us all courage to face each day. His radical, life-altering love undergirds us, giving us confidence to face the world outside our door with grace. That's the power of the gospel, both for our lives and our children's lives.

My prayer is that this book helps you fall in love again with Jesus, the Courageous and Confident One.

Part One:

Foundations

What does it mean to understand the world we live in? And how does that understanding affect our parenting? In this section, I'll discuss worldview and how it relates to everyday life. In a sense, I'll be dissecting our current mind-set, looking back to the world we grew up in as parents, and finding the gems and baubles of that perspective and today's. Welcome to the journey!

A Story

"Don't forget this." Jacob's mother shoved a tiny packet at his midsection, coarsely wrapped in brown paper. "You'll want to have hollyhocks in your new home—to attract a wife."

Jacob took the seeds. He smiled. "I'll need more than seeds, Mama, to attract a woman to the likes of *this*." He rubbed his stubbled face and looked at his parents. His entire life they seemed tall, looming even. Like the epic hemlocks guarding their claim, his parents sheltered him from relentless Pacific Northwest downpours. Today, though, he was unsettled to see how short Mama and Papa had become, how frail.

His father muffled words from the back of the cabin—marching orders. Whenever Papa mumbled, Jacob knew enough to hunker down and listen. The two shared a quiet camaraderie, so much so that Jacob knew to bring kindling to the stove where Papa stood. Without words, the once-mumbling man took each thin stick, broke it, and tossed it into the stove.

"Best be remembering everything we taught you," his father said.

"I've spent my life listening to you, Papa. You know that. I know how to milk a cow even when she's cross, how to survive in the woods for weeks at a time, how to plant corn and beans together like the Indians. I can skin a rabbit, start a fire from flint, and write a fine letter." Jacob wanted to thank his father then, but the words were held hostage on the tip of his tongue. There were things you didn't say to Papa, especially when he was sparking a fire in the stove.

Mama came behind Jacob now, stroking his shoulder. "Mind how you've been raised, Jacob-boy. You remember." She padded to the willow-tree rocking chair Papa had fashioned her when they were courting. She sat down. Her lips pursed as if they were ready to unleash a string of instructions. Instead, she took in a deep, autumn breath and rocked. Back and forth. Back and forth.

It was her way, Jacob knew. Mama's voice was more powerful when no words were uttered. In the silence, Jacob remembered the sentences Mama would have said. Should have said. *Work the farm when it is light; when it's dark, mend the tack. Remember the ant; store up your food for winter down in the cellar. Sleep the sleep of hard labor. When worry threatens, lift a prayer to the Almighty. Pioneering means taking risks. The dictionary spells good with two Os; the Bible spells it with one. All of life began in a garden; best keep cultivating. Feed the land when it's starving, let it lie fallow when it languishes, weed it when it's gangly.* All the words swirled through Jacob's heart, simultaneously stinging and blessing him. Growing up, becoming a man, was a beautiful and painful endeavor. Why did moving on mean leaving the two people who mattered most?

Surrounded by tendrils of nose-stinging wood smoke, Jacob coughed. He adjusted the satchel on his back, feeling its weight. His new life consisted of the leather bag's bulging contents: a knife, a bedroll, a gun, gunpowder, seeds from Mama's garden, a little money, hard tack for the journey, Papa's Bible, a *Farmer's Almanac,* woolen socks knitted days before, and all the hopes and aspirations of his parents. The hope—now etched on their lined faces—weighted him the most. All that hope poured into his life.

For this day.

He nodded to them both. He stood there many moments as the fire crackled to life, each hot sputter ticking away another agonizing moment. *Today's the day I leave them.* The words cadenced themselves in his head like a distant, constant drumbeat. Although distrustful of technology, Jacob suddenly wanted one of those picture boxes—to capture once and for all this moment, these faces that dared to ingrain their lives into his. But without a camera, Jacob had to click a picture of Mama and Papa in his mind, to imprint it permanently on the slate of his thoughts.

"Thanks," was all he said. One word. It seemed such a paltry word, so stripped of emotion, but it was all he had. If he let more words escape his dry mouth, he'd likely choke on his weeping. With that, he turned from them and opened the door, leaving his childhood in the embers of Papa's stove.

As soon as the heavy door thudded behind him, a strange odor assaulted his nostrils. Smoke. He lifted his eyes to see its hazy source— a screaming metal oxcart whirring by. In place of the treed world he grew to love was chaos, noise, clamor. The sun hinted at itself as glint on tall mirrored towers that seemed to hold the sky up. At Jacob's feet where mud should have clung to his soles was some sort of solid rock, strewn with bits of colored paper. People buzzed at him from all corners, from all places, pressing into him, looking at him with bewildered detachment.

It was his look as well. Bewildered. Detached. *Where am I?*

Jacob stomped his boots on the hard ground, hoping it would reorient him. No luck. Satchel still on his back, he stared down a central path teeming with men and women and children. Seeing a tall, metal hitching post, he willed himself to walk. As he approached what he now realized was a lamppost, he could feel the hardness of the trail jar his feet and knees. The screaming, smoke-emitting wagons passed by him, more insistent, louder than locomotives. He held the lamppost while the world screeched around him in a maniacal hurry. People, machines, tower-of-Babel buildings—all stung his eyes.

Jacob turned back, hoping he'd see the little cabin in the woods, chimney smoke kissing the clean sky, but it was gone. His parents and their gentle garden-loving ways were gone. Their voices grew quieter and quieter amid the cacophony until he could barely remember the tremor in his mother's song or the baritone richness of his father's lecture. He remembered his satchel then as he clung like a six-year-old to the lamppost.

Useless.

When he walked down the peopled street into the great, wild unknown, Jacob had no tools to navigate the world. He dropped his satchel and faced the confusing world lost and alone.

Two

A Need

I am sending you out like sheep among wolves, so be
wise as serpents and innocent as doves.

Matthew 10:16 net

This fictitious story should give us pause. Jacob's parents had every good intention. Within their world (dare I say worldview?), they prepared their son for life. They gave him the physical, spiritual, and emotional tools he needed to prosper in the world and navigate its twists and turns. The problem is, life changed. Utterly. Nothing his parents gave him was of any use. Through the mayhem of a stunningly new culture, his parents' voices blended into the noise, eventually disappearing altogether.

None of us wants to be like Jacob's well-meaning parents. Yes, we want to love our children and protect them from negative influences, but we don't want to do that to their detriment. Although I am quite comfortable living and breathing within a modern community, I want to look beyond the world of my home. I want to understand and see the story God is forcefully unfolding in the world today. I want to exegete culture as I exegete Scriptures—with thoughtful, learned observation, interpretation, and application. If, however, I shut the curtains to my cabin and refuse to see the changes, I am no different from Jacob's parents.

Why Do We Need to Understand Postmodernity?

- If we want to reach the world with the life-changing grace of Jesus Christ, we must understand it. If our hope and goal is to send our children out as His ambassadors, we owe it to them to teach them the culture into which they venture.

- Each worldview has its own jewels and baubles. Although mining modernity and postmodernity takes thought, prayer and work, we can uncover much about Jesus Christ from both perspectives. If our families cling to modernity and never question the genuineness of its baubles, we will never fully appreciate its jewels. If we reject postmodernity because of its baubles, we'll never experience its jewels.

- Rethinking how to present Jesus Christ to our children and to the world deepens our dependence on and relationship with Him. The words we've puppeted for years have lost their meaning. Reloading our speech with inviting ways to reveal Jesus is an invigorating spiritual exercise.

- Postmoderns see God's plan as a story of redemption, and all of us—parents and children—are active, engaged participants.

- Without an understanding of postmodernity, our methods will become wholly ineffective. Ivy Beckwith, author of *Postmodern Children's Ministry*, asserts, "We need to be thinking about new paradigms, new ways of doing what we're doing...If we don't, we'll soon find that we've become irrelevant to the families who live in the changing culture."[1]

- Understanding postmodern thought helps us engage with our children through narrative. Replacing three-point sermons with "That reminds me of a story" fosters relationship and intergenerational connection.

- Experiencing Jesus Christ—an important tenet for post-moderns—is richer than our oftentimes overly intellectual pursuit of Him. If we are seeking Jesus through our experience, our family will live with great anticipation. Brian McLaren applauds this seeking of honest, experiential Christianity, and his words on the subject have appropriate lessons for families. "The kind of experience we need more of is honest, unforced, and unhyped experience: honest feeling, uncensored, unedited, based on reflection, and honestly shared with others in stories."[2]

- Postmodernism's I-don't-have-all-the-answers paradigm spills over into parenting. The modern person's need for power and control (sometimes resulting in pride) is dissolved into humility. Perhaps parents really can learn from their children. This is essentially Dan Allender's thesis for his book *How Children Raise Parents*. He asserts, "Thank God for your children because they are the ones who grow you up into spiritual maturity. Far more than being concerned about how to correct, or convert, or counsel your children, thank God for what your children are teaching you."[3]

- Participating in community—another postmodern emphasis—alongside our children is a messy but ultimately satisfying experience. When we begin to understand that most of what Paul wrote to believers was written in the context of community—and not to individual, isolated Christians—we begin to see how oddly individualistic our language has become. "Jesus is in my heart," is replaced by "I experience Jesus' presence in the context of community." Understanding that much of what is written in the Bible for our instruction is directed at groups—not merely individuals—can revolutionize our reading of Scripture and our daily practice of it.

- Weaning ourselves from consumerism enhances family life. Psychologist Mary Pipher reveals, "The propaganda that life is made much happier by purchases encourages adults and children to make bad decisions about their time and money. Children alternate between the belief that products will make them happy and a deep cynicism about the promises of the adult world."[4] When families encourage gratitude instead of consumerism, they learn to enjoy each other, spend more time doing noncommercial outings together, rest easier in their financial situation, and appreciate the free beauty of God's creation.

- Becoming lifetime learners alongside your children produces camaraderie.

- Learning not to fear (or be threatened by) other's views on God and spirituality helps families become more hospitable and merciful toward those outside the faith.

The Neutrality of Postmodernism

Although parents might be tempted to tremble within their homes, postmodernity is neither malevolent nor magnificent. It is neutral. It is becoming the state of our workaday world. As parents raising children who will live, breathe, labor, marry, and raise our grandchildren in the context of postmodernity, we owe it to them to take a careful look at what it is as well as be cautious and humble learners.

As a fellow sojourner and a parent who doesn't have all the answers, I am beginning to see some benefits of postmodernity. I am realizing that some of what my modern upbringing taught me is antibiblical. And I am clinging to Jesus through the journey. I am learning that...

> Perhaps postmodernism has things to teach us as we parent. Perhaps this cultural shift is a blessing in disguise.

Perhaps emergent thinking will rejuvenate our relationship with God.

Perhaps this new paradigm, coupled with the life of Jesus, will revolutionize our families.

With that in mind, won't you join me as we seek to understand the postmodern paradigm?

Three

A Paradigm

If the title of this book intrigued you, you're most likely passionate about raising kids who understand their culture and then supersede it. Your job as a parent is to walk alongside your children and contextualize the culture for them. But what is this paradigm we live in? Before we can raise courageous and confident kids who succeed at what's important to them, we must first understand where we were and where we are today.

A Stroll down History Lane

Place yourself back in history class. Think back to AD 1700, when the age of reason dawned, the beginning of the modern age. The change happened over time. Little by little, people shifted their worldview. They began to see they could control parts of their worlds and even conquer countries. Man could control life. Machines made everyday living manageable. Science became the religion of the day as experimentation dissected the world into its smallest components.

Philosophically, folks began to shift their thinking, trading mysticism for logic, superstition for knowable truth. The individual reigned supreme. With unction, verve, and a desire to know all that is knowable, people found they could improve life, evolving until society's ills were eradicated. Humanity's newly discovered and amazing capabilities made God seem less and less important. Humankind's ability to solve any problem trumped the need for Him. Through reasoning ability, moderns could investigate and discover all absolute truth. Consequently, optimistic moderns believed in humanity's right to individually pursue happiness.

Other Modern Ideas

- More education creates a moral society.

- Skepticism is important. The miraculous cannot be proved.

- We make decisions in life based upon what we feel.

- We make decisions about choices if they make sense (utilitarianism).

- All knowledge is reachable by means of the mind.

- Atheism is logical.

- We can pull ourselves up by our bootstraps.

- "I think, therefore I am" (René Descartes).

- We can trust only what is proven through observation and experimentation (scientific rationalism).

- We can solve difficulties by analyzing them from different viewpoints.

- Thinking is linear. A + B = C.

- The needs of the individual supersede the needs of the community.

How Has Modernity Affected Christianity?

- We understand Christianity through factual research, based on an unshakable foundation of absolute truth.

- Apologetics (defending the faith) is a primary tool for helping people come to faith.

- Christianity is about "Jesus and me." He is our personal Lord and Savior.

- We come to Christ by means of a logical, measurable decision: "I walked the aisle when I was nine years old."

- Christians make decisions about life based on the way they feel and what God says to them personally.

A Cultural Shift in our Midst

The word *postmodernism* refers to a cultural shift our society has made over the past 50 years or so. *Postmodern* means "after modern." Therefore, it's a neutral term used to describe the state of flux we are currently experiencing. *Postmodern* isn't necessarily the opposite of *modern*; it's simply a shift in the way we process our worlds.

A modern person clings to facts and logic, but a postmodern person questions whether facts are always completely knowable and whether logic is always the best way to navigate life. Truth, to the postmodern mind, is not always objective (observable and knowable), but is often subjective (depending on circumstances). Perspective determines much of reality, and perspective, particularly cultural reality, shifts and changes from individual to individual. The individual is less prominent than the community in a postmodern society, and personal happiness is less important than the betterment of the community.

Other Postmodern Emphases

- Rationalism doesn't make a better society.

- Human ability is limited.

- Education doesn't necessarily make a better world.

- Deconstructionism is the new philosophy. In other words, many postmodern thinkers deny that one absolute truth undergirds all of life. However, some postmoderns would argue that they deconstruct old ways of thinking so they can build new, more helpful ways of thinking.

- Everyone's story is a part of a bigger narrative, but there are no longer any metanarratives, or universal stories, that universally define all cultures.

- Asking questions is helpful. Who are we? Where did we come from? Why are we here? Where are we going? What is right or wrong?

- Because no one truth is absolute, we cannot judge each other.

- Some elements of medieval mysticism or other ancient schools of thought are worth recovering.

- The transcendent is worth reaching for.

- Deep skepticism is often appropriate.

- What is real and what is not? The lines between the two are sometimes blurred.

- The ecology of the earth is of primary importance.

- The twin ideas of power and control are repulsive.

- Answers to life's questions are rarely simple or easily applied to every person's life. Life is messy and complicated, not easily dissected or understood.

How Does Postmodernity Affect the Church?

- Scripture primarily addresses the needs of the community.

- The validity of the Bible is sometimes questioned.

- Relationships are of primary importance.

- Postmoderns frequently seeking God in community rather than alone.

- Authenticity (being the same inside as how you appear on the outside) has become utterly important.

- Lone Ranger Christians have become a thing of the past.

- Postmodern evangelism is a process. The goal is not to convince someone to make a single and primarily rational decision.

- Discipleship occurs over years in community and seldom in a vacuum.

- Consumerism is to be guarded against, especially in the church.

- People filter their world through the curtain of story.

What Does This Mean for Parents?

How does all this line up with parenting courageous and confident kids? If you're like me, you have difficulty processing this new paradigm. Who cares if we've changed emphasis from the individual to the community? Why does it matter?

It matters because your children will grow up and live and work and love in a world with a worldview that is vastly different from the one in which you grew up.

As in the fictional story of Jacob at the beginning of this book, we will send our children into a world that is very different from their home. What can we do if their well-being depends on how we prepare them? How will they face their world with courage and confidence?

How do we parent when the world changes and moves at breakneck speed? Do we spend our time making knee-jerk reactions to every change? My fallback is Jesus. Simply trying to follow Him as we love our children is better than constantly reacting to the world around us. Mark Driscoll discusses the reactionary nature of postmodern thought:

Weary of conflict and war, postmodernity is a negative

reaction to modernity rather than a positive vision of a better alternative...Cultures, like homes, house people, and cultures unfit for residency need to be torn down like junk houses. But then an architect is needed to create a vision of something better or there will be a lot of people left homeless.[1]

The sticking point for parents is that we want to adequately prepare our children to live in a culture bent toward tearing things down and yet instill within them a hope for a better world.

Contextualization of the Gospel

Don Richardson, in his book *Eternity in Their Hearts*, discusses the idea of "redemptive analogies" set within each culture.[2] In every culture—and I would add, in every cultural viewpoint—God has given hints of Himself, fingerprints of His handiwork. Perhaps the key to navigating the minefield of cultural shift is understanding that God has redemptive analogies for us to discover about Him even now. We don't disdain one perspective over another. Rather, we see the greatness of God then and now, discerning how God actively intersects the culture outside our front doors.

Missionaries will tell you that the most important thing to do when immersing yourself in another country is to learn the language and the culture. Parenting today requires the same diligence. We need to understand the present culture precisely because if we don't, we might miss hints of God's redemptive analogy. We need to understand the language our culture speaks—not simply the words but also the nuances beneath the words.

We tend to disdain new culture and language, preferring the way we used to do things—a simple hallmark of a generation gap. But it's not either/or; it's both/and. We no longer throw out the baby with the bathwater. Instead, we keep the baby and change the bathwater. The gospel remains the same, but the presentation changes.

The Christian Cocoon

In the past 20 years, some Christian parents tended to cocoon their children from the big, bad world and to create Christian societies complete with their own clothing, music, movies, books, and so on. Instead of helping our children function in what we perceived as the evil culture, we barred our children from that culture and sheltered them. By doing this, we communicate this message: As long as you stay within our happy subculture, you'll be safe.

But how does that prepare our kids to face the world with confident courage? Too long we have mistaken protection for parenting.

Certainly, we are called by God, who entrusted our children to us, to protect, instruct, correct, and love them. We must allow them to be children as long as possible, shielding them from adult themes and nurturing their innocence. But like all journeys, the parent-child adventure changes over time. Sheltering gives way to instructing and eventually to releasing. In this way we are like a mother bird that brings worms to the nest, demonstrates the ease of flight to her birdlings, and then nudges them from the nest. You may be at the worm-finding stage, bundling your baby in warm blankets against the wind. Or you may be stooping low to the ground, once again demonstrating the art and skill of shoe tying to a finger-fumbling five-year-old. Maybe your heart races as your teenager hurtles and jerks your car while learning to drive. Children inevitably move from blankets to shoes to cars very quickly. And by the time they've progressed to cars, we pray that our teaching will find a permanent home in their hearts.

Preparing our children to find courage and confidence today requires a bit of everything—nurturing, teaching, releasing. To release our kids effectively, we must understand Jesus' mission. Throughout the book of John, we see the words *in the world*. The Father sent Jesus into our world. Jesus hung out with unsavory types, to the wrath of the religious leaders who considered such folk rabble. And yet He remained unstained by the world. That's the nuance we parents need to grasp—to engage as a family in people's lives in a way that beckons them to Jesus Christ *without* sacrificing our family to the world system. We must model and teach this to our children: Engage the culture yet remain unstained.

Jesus prayed this very thing in His high priestly prayer: "I have given them your word and the world has hated them, for they are not of the world any more than I am of the world. My prayer is not that you take them out of the world but that you protect them from the evil one" (John 17:14-15).

Engagement and Purity

James explains that true religion includes engaging and yet staying pure. He says, "Religion that God our Father accepts as pure and faultless is this: to look after orphans and widows in their distress [engaging the culture] and to keep oneself from being polluted by the world" (James 1:27).

The apostle Paul echoes this sentiment. "Do everything without complaining or arguing"—we could stop there, daring to apply that verse to our parenting—"so that you may become blameless and pure, children of God without fault in a crooked and depraved generation, in which you shine like stars in the universe" (Philippians 2:14-15). Imagine living as if we really believed that verse, as if we believed rubbing shoulders with the "evil world" need not defile us. According to James and Paul, we are to be vital parts of the world and yet still be blameless and innocent, shining as stars.

Training our children to thrive in this world includes empowering them to engage with the people who populate the world. "I have written you in my letter not to associate with sexually immoral people," Paul writes, "not at all meaning the people of this world who are immoral, or the greedy and swindler, or idolaters. In that case you would have to leave this world" (1 Corinthians 5:9-10). We've seen growth in our children as we've engaged with folks like this. We provide tools for their future interactions by demonstrating how to deal with the world on a daily basis.

When we lived stateside, we welcomed several Indian men into our lives. We loved those men, prayed for them, invited them into our home, and included them in our celebrations. One day, one of the men took our children into his bedroom and opened his closet. "These are my idols," he said. "I pray to them." Though we wouldn't have chosen to expose our children to these frightening images, the experience did provide a learning opportunity. We talked about idolatry and how Americans have idols too, though they look quite a bit different. The children prayed more for the Indian men as a result, and they continued to love them, listen to them, and play with them.

"Now this is our boast," Paul says. "Our conscience testifies that we have conducted ourselves in the world, and especially in our relations with you, in the holiness and sincerity that are from God. We have done so not according to worldly wisdom but according to God's grace" (2 Corinthians 1:12). Paul invested in people, yet his heart remained pure. His words and actions instruct us about being near God while conducting ourselves in the world.

Abram, before he became a father to many, understood this relationship between pursuing God and engaging people. When God told Abram to leave everything and follow Him to a new place, Abram obeyed. "From there he went on toward the hills east of Bethel and pitched his tent, with Bethel on the west and Ai on the east. There he built an altar to the LORD and called on the name of the LORD" (Genesis 12:8). Oswald Chambers illuminates the beauty of the location where Abram pitched his tent. "Bethel is the symbol of communion with God; Ai is the symbol of the world. Abraham pitched his tent between the two."[3]

As parents walking with our children through a postmodern paradigm, this concept of pitching our tents between communion with God and engagement in the world should encourage us. If we don't point our children toward the God of the universe, they miss out on the beauty of knowing and loving Him. Likewise, if we neglect showing them how to engage in the world outside our church's doors, they miss out on the beauty of knowing and loving the people God created. We've been told we are in the world but not of the world. That calls for engagement, for interaction—on both levels. We must engage God and interact with Him, and we must engage the culture and interact with it. Doing both—together and simultaneously—leads to spiritual growth and maturity.

We have friends heading to Sweden to be missionaries. In their prayer letter, they highlighted a new clothing line:

> A Swedish designer named Bjorn Atldax is selling a new label of jeans in Sweden called Cheap Monday. The jeans, while being popular for their trendy fit and low price, also serve another purpose other than fashion. The designer, Atldax, in a statement to the Associated Press, claims the jeans' logo of a skull with a cross turned upside down on its forehead is, in his words, "an active statement against Christianity." His proclaimed intention is to make young people question Christianity, which he describes as "a force of evil that has sparked wars throughout history."[4]

With that in mind, and with three girls heading into a culture that doesn't seem fazed by Atldax, the Mills family role-played a scene at their dinner table. "In our pretend scenario," Renee Mills wrote, "the girls were approached by a new little Swedish friend sporting a brand-spankin' new pair of Cheap Monday jeans. As you can imagine, this prompted a good family discussion on ways in which to stay true to our Savior while also loving our neighbor."[5] The jeans weren't the issue. They proved to be a vehicle the Mills family used to talk about how to love people with different values. This family is preparing to walk that sometimes blurry line between loving God and engaging culture.

After several months in France, I asked Sophie, "What have you learned about God in the past eight months in France that you didn't know before?"

"That's a hard one," she said. After a bit of thought, she answered, "Well, I now know that the world is more than the United States. I really only thought of the world in terms of that. I realize how selfish I was to do that. The world is much bigger." She paused. "I also realized that God is everywhere, not only in America."

"Sophie," I said, "that is a lesson many of us have a hard time learning."

She replied, "In Texas, all my friends were Christians, and most people we knew were Christians. It's been really different to meet people who don't know Jesus at all."

Sophie's authenticity humbled me. I marveled at her ability to articulate the things God taught her through interaction with friends who don't yet know Him. How ironic—I had worried incessantly about how her peers would affect her relationship with God. I wondered if exposing her to the world would hinder her heart toward Jesus. Instead, she's grown up a bit, coming to an understanding of the world few seldom grasp—that God loves this entire planet full of people and that—surprise!—He's not an American.

It Boils Down to Heart

It's not what goes into the heart that messes us up, it's what comes out. Jesus said so after He rebuked the Pharisees for lacking authenticity and demonstrating hypocrisy. He quoted Isaiah 29:13 to them first: "These people honor me with their lips, but their hearts are far from me. They worship me in vain; their teachings are but rules taught by men" (Matthew 15:8-9). Then He said, "What goes into a man's mouth does not make him 'unclean,' but what comes out of his mouth, that is what makes him 'unclean'" (verse 11).

Could it be that we parents have missed Jesus' central teaching? That we've manipulated our worlds so that nothing can defile our children, all the while forgetting that we've neglected nurturing our children's hearts? Or that in neglecting to engage the people of the world (not the world's system), we deny our children valuable life lessons?

I'm reminded of a family I knew once. The parents were hypervigilant about what they allowed their children to watch on television. (I'm not saying this is wrong; we monitor our children's media as well.) They created all sorts of rules about what they could and could not do, eat, and see. But like the religious leaders Jesus rebuked, much of their Christianity became words, not heart. These parents knew all the right words to say to sound holy. But their hearts were far from God.

You'd think by protecting their children from the outside world, they'd be protecting their children's hearts. Instead, their children caught their hypocritical approach to Christianity. They obeyed the exterior rules, but their hearts resembled their parents'. One day one of my children came home from a visit to their house and said, "I don't want to go back."

"Why?"

"Because they yell and scream all the time. Please don't make me go back there."

From the outside, everything appeared normal. But my child's perspective from the inside was much different.

So much of our parenting depends upon our hearts first. If we are far from Jesus, our pretense will rub off on our children, regardless of how many religious rules we impose. Today's savvy children—who are quick to question everything—watch the way we chart our course through a rapidly changing world, where maps that help us navigate life change weekly. They want to see whether we're authentic. Not perfect, but authentic. We may yell and say things we regret. But an authentic and humble parent admits these things openly. He doesn't pretend he's got it all together. She doesn't blame her outbursts on her children.

Our children will be bombarded with the idea that everything, beliefs notwithstanding, is suspect—particularly morality, truth, and authority. They are taught to question authority. Rebellion is applauded as a natural rite of passage. We must live our lives in such a way before our children that they know we are actively pursuing relationship with Jesus and with them. And that what we say is what we mean. They need to see us struggle and wrestle. They need to see Christianity lived out on the playing field of our families, to see the redemptive hand of God in our lives and how that gives us the courageous confidence to face the world each day.

Phil and Laina, who are parenting five kids in Europe as they start a new community of believers, understand this. One evening around their dinner table, they discussed an invitation. Their eldest daughter had been invited to spend a weekend with friends in another city with no parental supervision.

"I knew what choice I wanted my daughter to make," Laina said, "but I chose to listen to her." For the next several minutes, they had a frank talk about sex and drugs and unsupervised weekends. A friend of theirs was visiting, listening wide-eyed to the conversation. "It wasn't an easy conversation," Laina said, "but Phil and I thought it best to let our daughter express everything so we could hear her process this choice. Eventually, she chose not to go because her closest friend, who would have been her only support, wasn't able to go."

They wrestled through the decision in the context of authenticity. "If I had told her no right at the beginning, that would have ended the conversation. We long for our children to be able to create their own decision-making grid so they can establish their own healthy boundaries." Through a hearty discussion, Laina's daughter made a good decision while enjoying emotional closeness with her parents.

Parenting in the Change

Parenting in the midst of the cultural change, particularly as postmodern thought replaces modern thought, is a difficult task best tackled with hefty doses of engaging God, embracing people, and seeking to be authentic heart-followers of Jesus. As parents, we walk the journey we want our children to walk, paving it with our genuine struggles and victories along the way. As we do, our children learn to be courageous, settled in their relationship with Jesus. And as they engage their world with Jesus' help, confidence blossoms.

Four

A New Tradition

Steep your life in God-reality, God-initiative, God-provisions. Don't worry about missing out. You'll find all your everyday human concerns will be met.

MATTHEW 6:33 MSG

Life. It's not about me. Or you. Or our children. This life we've been given—the life we savor once and like a vapor is gone—is about Jesus. Somewhere in the muddle of evaluating the modern perspective or correctly dissecting postmodernity, we've missed that central, simple truth. Life's not about us. This is the single most important truth we must communicate with our children as they venture into a world of postmodern thought. Jesus is what it's all about. He is the once upon a time and the happily ever after of their stories—the Alpha and Omega of our children's lives.

So how do we show Jesus to our children? How do we parent in such a way that invites the mystery of Jesus into their daily lives? And how will this help our children face the big, bad world, where wolves howl violent song lyrics and thieves lurk in Internet chat rooms? Where relativism and lascivious behavior are applauded?

We reveal Jesus by modeling Him. By inviting Him to be near. By muddying our knees in prayer with our children. By walking through life with our children in a tandem dance of discipleship. By lifting our children's gaze from this crazy world to the real world—the kingdom of God.

Seek His Kingdom First

Jesus spoke these simple yet difficult words: "But seek first his kingdom and his righteousness, and all these things will be given to you as well" (Matthew 6:33). I've often sought answers, particularly parenting answers. I grew up in a home I didn't want to duplicate, so I ran here and there, seeking the right parenting methods. In a way, I was lost, so I sought. After several years of seeking solace in methods and raising my kids by formula, I realized I'd missed out on a vital component of parenting—connectivity to Jesus. Parenting strategies are some of the "things" Jesus can add to us, but first we must see the condition. Notice the verse starts with a perplexing word: *but*. It means that our tendency as humans is to do anything *but* seek Jesus. He tells us to lay aside our frenetic search for stuff and instead seek Him, His kingdom, and His righteousness.

The verse continues though.

"Therefore do not worry about tomorrow, for tomorrow will worry about itself. Each day has enough trouble of its own" (Matthew 6:34). In this paradigm-changing world, where modernity bows to postmodernity, parents are anxious. We worry about our children, how they will be when they breathe the air outside our doors. We wonder if we're preparing them for the future, whether they'll be ready to face a world of relativity. We tend to raise children out of fear and anxiety—to protect them from the evils crouching in this world. But Jesus tells us to shed anxiety, to quell fear—a seemingly impossible request.

We need to see that the two verses above are linked. Seek Jesus; shed anxiety. Run to Him; flee from fear. Point to the kingdom; trust He'll order your little kingdom of children, even if He takes longer than you envisioned.

Obey God

These verses, along with the leading of Jesus, helped me do what I thought was an impossible thing—raise my children in a country where less than one-half of one percent know Jesus, where postmodernity reigns and God is considered irrelevant and intrusive. Before we moved from the safety of our happy Dallas enclave to the wild, woolly recesses of France, I worried. I fretted. How would my children turn out in such a culture? Would they hate me? Would my obedience to Jesus cost them their faith? I read words like these:

> If we obey God, it is going to cost other people more than it costs us, and that is where the sting comes in…We can disobey God if we choose, and it will bring immediate relief to the situation, but we shall be a grief to our Lord. Whereas if we obey God, He will look after those who have been pressed into the consequences of our obedience. We have simply to obey and leave all the consequences with Him.[1]

I wanted to gather my three children, sheltering them in a safe embrace. And yet God called Patrick and me to obey Him, to follow His leading to a new and difficult place. In my stress, I begged Jesus to embrace my children. I prayed I'd be able to leave all the consequences with Him.

A Difficult Leap into Postmodernity

We moved thousands of miles away from security and familiarity to the land of French wine and cheese. I will never forget the day we enrolled our two youngest children in French schools. My stomach was filled with butterflies as we walked Aidan and Julia two blocks toward their elementary school, a walk that felt more like a funeral procession than a parade. I felt the crushing guilt of putting my children through such a difficult trial. How would I be able to let them go, to release them to Jesus?

Standing in the courtyard, parents milling around me, I wondered again about my parenting, about my sanity, bringing my children to such a place. Jesus' words about worry played hide-and-seek far away in my mind. I could only remember the "Seek first the kingdom" part, and that was nearly making me sick.

I would have been fine if it hadn't been for those brown eyes.

Spotlighted by the sun while she stood small in the courtyard, blonde-headed Julia stared at me with a mixture of fear, excitement, and abandonment. As tears pooled in the recesses of her big browns, mine had to look away briefly. *But seek first His kingdom and His righteousness.*

"You'll do great, Julia. Watch everyone else. When someone takes out a pencil, you take out a pencil."

She nodded and took a deep breath, the tears trapped within their lidded boundaries, as if we both knew if she let them dribble down her tanned cheek, we'd be done for. We would have allowed the fear and pain of the moment to get the most of us.

So we stood there, we two, in the middle of a paved schoolyard in a small French village, wondering what the day would hold for her. Anxiety circled my heart. I sucked in a breath and lifted Julia to myself in a protective mother embrace. As long as she stayed cocooned, wrapped in my arms, she would be safe.

But then her non-English-speaking teacher, who had an edge about her that unsettled me, clapped her hands. Automatically, the children—including Julia—lined up in rows of two. They grabbed the hands of their partners—I was later to learn my Julia's partner was a little bully girl also named Julia—and they marched into the school building to the applause and waves of their parents.

I didn't applaud.

I did wave.

I wiped my eyes that dared to spill tears Julia bravely held in.

I will always remember the way her brown eyes begged me that first day of school, how they pierced my mommy heart from behind blonde bangs. She kept looking backward as she held the other Julia's hand, pleading silently. *Take me back home, Mommy,* her eyes said. *I don't know what anyone is saying. I'm afraid. Please don't leave me here.*

If I hurried, I had enough time to find Aidan before he went into the classroom. But I was too late. Patrick and I stood outside his classroom while Aidan sat at a desk, looking straight ahead.

"He's trying not to cry," Patrick said.

Another set of brown eyes—large and looming like his father's—looked at me with the same mixture of fear and fretting. Aidan sucked in shallow breaths, his shoulders heaving, trying very hard not to cry. Even from a distance, I could see red encircling his eyes as his lower lip protruded. He was sitting alone. I'm sure he felt alone.

The night before, I told Julia and Aidan the story of Peter walking on water.[2] "When Peter looked into Jesus' eyes," I told them, "the Lord did amazing things." I asked them if they had ever walked on water. Both shook their heads.

"Going to a school where hardly anyone speaks your language is kind of like walking on water," I said. "You gotta keep your eyes on Jesus, and He will keep you afloat."

I asked them what happened next in the story.

"Peter sank because he looked at the wind and the sea," Aidan said.

"You're right," I explained, "but that's not the point of the story."

They stared at me with those big browns, wondering.

"Even when Peter looked away from Jesus' eyes and started sinking, Jesus still extended His hand to Peter and rescued him." I pulled my youngest two close. "That's the way it is for you. Jesus will be with you in school. And even if things get hard and you look at all the worries around you and feel like you're sinking, He will find you and lift you up." *And all these things will be given to you as well.*

Then, that morning, as I watched Aidan's chest heave, I wondered what was going on in his head. His brown eyes and the eyes of his sister bored a hole in my soul. But as I stood on the hot pavement, I knew the eyes of Jesus were on my children too.

And He would not let them sink.

My friend Kate said it well. "We realized that our children would be better able to tackle any problem now that they've gone through cultural transition in France." It's true. All that maternal worry and fear I clung to has dissolved into the beauty of seeing my children become better able to deal with life. God did that. He took our children, who were pressed into the consequences of our obedience, and did miracles. He showed up. He calmed my anxiety. He added the strength I needed to parent in a hyper-postmodern context, where my children hear that creation by God is ridiculous and practicing séances is cool, in a country boasting more mediums and spiritists than evangelical pastors.

So through the jumble of parenting in a shifting culture, cling to Jesus' simple truth. Seek His kingdom. Trust. Dare not to be anxious. Point your children to the life of Christ residing dynamically within you.

The moment I finished typing these words, Melanie e-mailed me, saying this:

> More and more the world is going to need people who are truly like Jesus. To prepare our kids for a postmodern world, we need to teach them about the importance of discipleship and being Jesus to the world over what my parents stressed growing up—attending church "every time the doors were open." How can I teach my son to discern sin, love the sinner, resist temptation, and be Jesus to everyone?[3]

It's an important question. Many modern parenting tomes approach the art of child-rearing as if by a formula. Do this, and kids will turn out this way. Follow these strategies, and your children will obey. Find the best Sunday school or youth group or summer camp to maximize your children's chances of following Christ when they leave the house.

Parenting by Braille

My friend Laina, whom I mentioned earlier, likens postmodern parenting to what she calls "parenting by braille."

"I parent by touch," she said. "By feel. All I can do sometimes is reach for Jesus when I am not sure how to figure out parenting. He shows me what to do along the way." This organic approach has helped Phil and Laina parent their children in a society embracing everything and anything but Christianity. "I want to pursue the souls of my children," Laina said, "to let them know they can be themselves, to give them that freedom." The result? Her children go to her with their complex issues. They trust a mom who parents by braille, who cheers for them while begging Jesus to give her wisdom, who is willing to admit she doesn't have all the answers. "We have worked hard at asking good questions rather than giving right answers," her husband, Phil, added.

Shifting our thinking from a formulaic step-by-step method to walking blindly with Jesus through the adventure of parenting is not easy. Jesus never promised that following Him down narrow paths was undemanding. Peter left his livelihood, exchanging stability for uncertainty, following a carpenter who claimed He was the Son of God. Paul had to shed his religion to follow Jesus. He faced persecution for the rest of his life. What makes us think that following Jesus as we parent will be any different?

Truth Is a Person

Much is made these days about truth, particularly the term *absolute truth*. We should be concerned that absolutes are under attack, but I'm reminded of this: Jesus is The Truth. He is truth on legs, truth personified. If we want absolute truth, we absolutely need Jesus.

Following hard after Him should be our highest goal, even more than parenting perfectly, because life is not about us. It's about Him.

The more we press to know Jesus and His countercultural ways, the more of His DNA we'll impart to our children. Many have said that childrearing is caught, not taught, and that our children will more likely imitate our actions than listen to our words. I knew a family once where the parents taught about humility and servanthood, but they lived as if they were privileged because they were leaders. When the parents lost their leadership position, did the children respond with humility as their parents had taught them? Were they thankful for the opportunity to simply serve? No. They flung themselves on the floor weeping because a position was taken away. They followed their parents' actions, ignoring their words.

What those parents didn't understand was that parenting is an inside-out phenomenon. What is inside us flows out into our children.

We can implement formulas, tell all the right stories, do the required amount of family devotions, and still be imparting exactly the opposite of what we teach. If our outsides (what we say) don't match the insides (how we act or really feel), our children will detect the difference and will act accordingly. That's why we must make sure our hearts are right. The best method for parenting in a postmodern context is to be real, to share struggles, to show how you run to Jesus when disappointment strikes. Parenting, boiled down to its essence, is modeling. How you want your children to be on the inside must match your own insides—and your insides need to be surrendered to the kingdom of God.

What is the goal of parenting as postmodernity kicks at our heels? Producing perfect children who fit into our American box of Christianity (which leans far more toward commercialism and materialism than we're willing to admit)? Or is it to raise children who are infatuated with the person of Jesus, who know life's not all about them?

A Unique Perspective

Mark Driscoll, pastor and author of *The Radical Reformission*, developed a unique perspective on what our goal should be as followers of Christ. Consider his words in light of parenting your children: "I learned that God's mission is not to create a team of moral and decent people but rather to create a movement of holy loving missionaries who are comfortable and truthful around lost sinners and who, in this way, look more like Jesus than most of his pastors do."[4]

Sophie, our eldest, is becoming a follower of Jesus who is comfortable and truthful around lost sinners. A few months into school on French soil, mean girls started teasing her. When she fell headlong into a field, muddying her pants during PE class, one of the girls said, "Look at that American. She's a baby. She fell." Later, those same girls scrawled a mean comment about one of Sophie's friends on a school wall. Sophie's friends, who don't yet know Christ, wanted revenge. Sophie said, "If we return the favor, they will too. It's better to forgive." That evening as Sophie recounted the day, she talked about her struggle to love the mean girls. "It's really hard to love your enemies," she said.

Sophie was surrounded by wealthy students. She often heard kids say, "My dad makes so much money," or "We're buying a second home." This is followed by, "What does your dad do?" Sophie answered honestly, but I could tell she had a twinge of pain, the kind of pain that wanted her daddy to have the same kind of job he had in the States. When she said, "My dad's a pastor," one of the girls laughed at her. When we secured our church office, she seemed relieved. Her daddy had a real job.

Aidan had his own battle. He was troubled by the emphasis on evolution in his class. He came home one day and said, "I heard the goofiest thing today. Our teacher thinks we came from apes." But then he had a test over the information presented in class, and the night before, he was in conflict. He is a good student and wanted to do well on his test, but he didn't want to answer the questions with answers about evolution. We prayed for him. Late that night, I climbed the ladder to his bunk bed and prayed for him again. Our cat, Madeline, who always knows which child or adult needs her the most, was curled around his legs.

Julia's teacher yelled at her. Julia didn't know why. Then the teacher took her chair and put her in the hall for "a long time" according to our daughter. And Julia's turncoat friend was at it again. She took Julia's things—the snack we give her each day, her prized cache of marbles—and didn't return them. One morning, Aidan said, "I'm keeping Julia's snack and marbles in my backpack. I hope Julia and I have the same recess so I can give these to her when she needs them."

Our dear, sweet boy is becoming a man, protecting his sister from a bully. When Julia heard Aidan's protective words, she threw her arms around him and thanked him.

Julia asked her classmates if they knew God. "Mom," she said. "No one really knows God in my school." Still, she kept telling them.

Little by little, our children are learning to follow Jesus down His kingdom path. They're learning life's not all about them. Though

Patrick and I often feel that we—like Laina—are parenting by braille, we were encouraged to see our children had hearts like Jesus in the midst of a very difficult school environment. It gave me hope that perhaps this inside-out, kingdom-minded parenting thing is working on a heart level. That training and mentoring our children is preparing them for a postmodern world that desperately needs to know Truth personified.

Five

The Truth

Truth has stumbled in the streets,
honesty cannot enter.

Isaiah 59:14

"What is truth?" Pilate asked.[1] Pilate was part philosopher, part puppet of Rome, and our words today echo his. Perhaps the biggest debate currently raging in Christian circles is focused on the nature of truth. Can we know absolute truth? If we can't, what kind of foundation can we expect to build our lives or our families on?

Before we explore the concept of truth, we need to grasp how central the concept of truth is in Scripture:

- The word *truth* is mentioned 228 times, more than *hope* (174) and slightly less than *joy* (242) and *peace* (247).
- God is called the God of truth (Psalm 31:5; Isaiah 65:16).
- Truth protects (Psalm 40:11).
- Truth guides us into God's presence: "Send forth your light and your truth, let them guide me; let them bring me to your holy mountain, to the place where you dwell" (Psalm 43:3).
- God speaks the truth (Isaiah 45:19).
- We are told to love truth (Zechariah 8:19).

- Jesus said "I tell you the truth" 82 times.

- Jesus is the Word, who "became flesh and made his dwelling among us. We have seen his glory, the glory of the One and Only, who came from the Father, *full of grace and truth*" (John 1:14).

- Jesus said He is the truth (John 14:6).

- The Holy Spirit is called the Spirit of truth (John 14:17; 15:26; 16:13; 1 John 5:6).

- Love "rejoices with the truth" (1 Corinthians 13:6).

- Truth is an integral part of our spiritual armory: "Stand firm then, with the belt of truth buckled around your waist" (Ephesians 6:14).

- The gospel is called the truth (Colossians 1:6).

- The church is the foundation of truth (1 Timothy 3:15; 4:3).

- We can come to the knowledge of the truth (Romans 2:20; 1 Timothy 2:4; 2 Timothy 2:25; Titus 1:1; Hebrews 10:26).

- Truth leads to godliness (Titus 1:1).

This short list should spark a fire in our hearts to value truth. After all, as parents we deeply value truth in our children. When our children lie to us, we take it more seriously than a simple act of disobedience. A strong home is a home where truth reigns, where grace permeates the atmosphere of our homes so that our children feel comfortable speaking the truth.

Absolute Truth

I consider myself part of the emerging culture—a postmodern—but I am uncomfortable with some of the emergent ramblings about absolute truth. I understand that humanity comprehends truth through the filter of culture, but I can't let go of the fact that truth—in its purest, God-breathed form—exists and should be highly valued. The God of truth founded this world in which we breathe.

Jesus, God's Son, said He is truth, that if you looked directly at Him, you'd see truth with skin on. He said, "I am the way and the truth and the life. No one comes to the Father except through me" (John 14:6). Jesus is truth personified. And He, along with the Father and the Holy Spirit, created the earth. The apostle Paul leaves no wiggle room when he writes, "For by him all things were created: things in heaven and on earth, visible and invisible, whether thrones or powers or rulers or authorities; all things were created by him and for him. He is before all things, and in him all things hold together" (Colossians 1:16-17).

Jesus, the truth, holds all things together. The world spins on its axis for Him. The world spins on its axis because of Him. We walk this earth for Him. We walk this earth because of Him. All of life boils down to Him, our central truth.

We All Miss the Truth

Moderns have missed this. Postmoderns miss this too. Many moderns seem to consider truth to be abstract, logical, and attainable, and they fail to realize that Jesus in all His God-man complexity is more like untamed Aslan—we can know him, certainly, but we cannot package and market him. And many postmoderns seem to ramble on and on about words and meanings, forgetting that the ultimate meaning comes through relationship with Jesus. Of course, I am oversimplifying. Certainly, many moderns run hard after the untamed Lion just as many postmoderns cling to truth without bending to theological liberalism.

As parents trying to understand this culture shift, though, we do well to understand exactly where we are in our understanding of truth. Whatever we believe, we will pass, overtly or subliminally, to our children, who will then use what we have taught them as a filter through which they view all of life.

Obedience and Freedom

Seeing truth in the context of simple obedience to Jesus transcends both postmodernity and modernity. Regardless of the culture we find ourselves in, Jesus' mandate is always the same. "Follow me," He said to an ancient culture. He breathed that to a modern culture, and He beckons with the same words to our current culture. The fascinating part about knowing truth as the person of Jesus Christ is that, in some odd way, we can measure how much we know it.

How exactly is truth measurable? Through freedom.

Consider Jesus' words: "If you hold to my teaching, you are really my disciples. Then you will know the truth, and the truth will set you free" (John 8:31-32). Some of us are guilty of coupon-clipping the Bible. We cut in half verses that are supposed to be together so we can keep the happy parts and discard the difficult. But we can't clip away the difficult obedience aspect of Christianity from the happy freedom that obedience produces. Jesus said that if we obey His teaching, we will not only understand truth, we will be set free by it. This is paradoxical to be sure, but it's liberating. Follow Jesus. Be set free.

The old hymn text "Trust and Obey" by John H. Sammis comes to mind. "Trust and obey, for there's no other way to be happy in Jesus but to trust and obey." As we truly follow Jesus, we find this to be true. He says, "Come to me, all you who are weary and burdened, and I will give you rest. Take my yoke upon you and learn from me, for I am gentle and humble in heart, and you will find rest for your souls" (Matthew 11:28-29). When we follow, Jesus gives us rest and sets us free from anxieties.

Parenting from the Proverbs

The same dynamic occurs in our homes. Our children are happier if they choose to follow *us* and heed our God-infused advice. Obedience to the truth brings a blessing. The Proverbs are full of wisdom-permeated nuggets like these:

- "Listen, my son, to your father's instruction and do not forsake your mother's teaching. They will be like a garland to grace your head and a chain to adorn your neck" (Proverbs 1:8-9). Notice how obedience is tied to beauty or adornment. Listen and heed your parents, receive beauty. What a compelling picture of the merits of obeying.

- "My son, if you accept my words and store up my commands within you, turning your ear to wisdom and applying your heart to understanding, and if you call out for insight and cry aloud for understanding, and if you look for it as for silver and search for it as for hidden treasure, then you will understand the fear of the LORD and find the knowledge of God" (Proverbs 2:1-5). How do our children know God? By obeying their parents. The same is true for us. How do we obtain that elusive fear of God? By obeying Him.

- "My son, do not forget my teaching, but keep my commands in your heart, for they will prolong your life many years and bring you prosperity" (Proverbs 3:1-2). Having a prosperous soul—a goal any parent wants for his children—comes from remembering and keeping a parent's wise counsel.

- "Listen, my son, accept what I say, and the years of your life will be many. I guide you in the way of wisdom and lead you along straight paths. When you walk, your steps will not be hampered; when you run, you will not stumble" (Proverbs 4:10-12). Accepting what parents say enables a child to live life fully with fewer pitfalls and more freedom.

- "Stop listening to instruction, my son, and you will stray from the words of knowledge" (Proverbs 19:27). Again,

this shows that obedience is tied to knowing truth—
that if we fail to obey, we will have difficulty understanding truth. Keep in mind, though, that God's sovereignty
is bigger than our frailty. Though we fall and make myr-
iads of mistakes, God is never finished with us. He can
take our foibles and teach us through them.

Truth, then, is never found in a vacuum. We grow in truth as we
obey. Our children grow in their knowledge of the truth as they obey
us. And the ultimate result of all that obedience is freedom.

Freedom and Truth

I'm fascinated that in the account of the stronger and weaker
brother (1 Corinthians 8–9), the stronger brother is the one with
more freedom. The closer we get to Jesus (and the closer our families
move toward Him), the freer we become.

We've seen this principle in operation in our home. Julia came
home from school, seemingly happy. But as we sat around the dinner
table and shared our highs and lows from the day, her story of sadness
eventually spilled out. "My teacher made fun of me," she said. "I'm
stupid." When the time came for her to do her homework, she cried,
"I don't want to do it. I don't understand it!"

Finally, Patrick realized that we weren't helping her situation by
simply battling her to do her homework. "Come sit down with me,"
he told her. He patted the couch.

"No," she said.

"Come on, Julia. I'm here to help you."

She sat next to him. After a long discussion, Patrick figured out
that Julia was struggling to learn and memorize her French verb tenses.

"But I'm stupid," she said.

"No, you're not. It just takes practice. I'm here to help you." Patrick
got out a piece of paper and started writing out her verb tenses.

After an hour of instruction, Julia smiled. And jumped. And
laughed again. Once she listened to and heeded Patrick's advice, she

not only understood French verbs better but also experienced freedom. She'd been locked in a prison of feeling stupid, only to be set free by a wise, loving father.

The day of her verb test, Julia smiled at me. "Mommy, this is going to be the best day ever."

"Why?"

"Because I know my verbs. I'm smart. My teacher will be so proud of me."

Had we berated her for her disdain for homework, I know we wouldn't have heard those happy words. Had we clung to control for the sake of being her authority instead of coming alongside her and imparting bits of truth, she would be imprisoned, a seed of rebellion growing in her heart.

What would our families look like if freedom rather than control measured how well we were following truth? As we parent from infant to toddler to child to young adult, could we see more freedom as our children age? Less adherence to legalism and more capacity to actually walk a faith journey with Jesus?

Growing in freedom through obedience is one aspect of understanding truth. Another, though, is discerning truth in such a way that we don't overintellectualize the gospel.

Wrangling About Words Versus Living the Word

I've been reading a lot of postmodernity books as I've prepared to write this book. One book about the church and postmodernity made me mad. For a long time I couldn't figure out why. Now I know. I'm intrigued by the voices of those crying in the wilderness, calling for change from the pews of our traditional modern churches. And yet something unsettled me.

Here it is: Jacob.

A friend of mine has a dear son named Jacob who lives with a brain injury. The few times I've seen him, I have met pieces of Jesus. He understands the gospel in a simple way yet more profoundly than I ever will. My friend sometimes shares stories about him on her blog, how he doesn't seem to care that his voice is louder than anyone else's during worship, how he laughs when he's happy, how he truly, truly loves Jesus. His mother, Jeanne, writes these insightful words:

> The most remarkable thing about Jacob now is his faith, which radiates from him with such intensity one can only wonder what fellowship he shared with his Father during those months of darkness. When he worships, it's as though he's standing face to face with the Lord. I've seen total strangers watch him and weep. And yet, for a long time I struggled with all Jacob had lost—the brilliant mind, the beautiful musical gifts, the physical coordination. I couldn't understand why God would heal him partway and leave him with so many deficits. One day when I was praying about it, I sensed God speaking to my heart and asking me what I wanted most for my children. I answered, "That when they stand in Your presence, You will say, Well done, good and faithful servant." God reminded me how Jacob's faith touches so many. It was as though He said, "Jacob is my good and faithful servant. I am satisfied in him. I want you to be too." As parents we aspire to great things for our kids. Jacob taught me to keep my eye on the one most important goal."[2]

That's what bothers me about all the pontificating. It's as if we've lost Jesus in the midst of our very intellectual discussions about postmodernity. We've divorced ourselves from modern tradition, from Scriptural authenticity. But instead of being anchored, we float around discussing paradigms and community and mystery. We use lots of really smart words to define Christianity. We make it appealing to thinkers while Jacob flings his arms heavenward and simply adores his Savior.

I'm a thinker. I enjoy discourse. But I wonder whether we are forgetting this verse in our intellectual meanderings about truth: "But I am afraid that just as Eve was deceived by the serpent's cunning, your minds may somehow be led astray from your sincere and pure devotion to Christ" (2 Corinthians 11:3).

The serpent has a way with words. He is able to sway minds. He rallies against simplicity and purity of devotion. He must watch Jacob and utterly cower. And all the while we write and talk and parent, using words but not living them out. I worry that we've already been deceived and that Paul's words aptly reflect this current generation of Christians: "They exchanged the truth of God for a lie, and worshipped and served created things rather than the Creator—who is forever praised. Amen" (Romans 1:25).

I love that we are shifting from modernity to postmodernity. I love the new adventure for families as we navigate the shift. I love that some of our surfacy modern structures are crumbling in favor of deeper, authentic spirituality. But sometimes I don't enjoy the discourse because it feels as if we're exchanging the beauty of God's truth for a lie. It wearies me. It makes me feel as if I'm floating without an anchor, without a firm foundation of truth and simple faith.

Does hyperintellectual Christianity change the world? Does it impact the kingdom? Why do I leave a book like the one I read last night with confusion and despair, yet when I look at Jacob's face I want to be more like Jesus?

Jesus is a person. He is more than mind. He is even more than words. Perhaps we do Him a disservice if we allow our minds to intellectualize everything. I preach this to myself. I love words, making a living from them. But I don't want to be led astray from the simplicity and purity of devotion to Jesus. I don't want to forget Him—He who rescued me from myself, sin, hell.

Once someone asked Bill Bright in an interview what he felt about Jesus. He broke down and wept. I pray I break down and weep if I am asked that question—that my heart would be so knitted to His, so grateful for His life, that all I can do is weep. Or maybe laugh.

I want to be like Jacob.

My friend Leslie tells of a similar encounter. At a youth camp, a girl named Ellen who had Down syndrome sat alone in the cafeteria. Leslie and her husband saw her there as she rocked gently back and forth, and they asked if they could sit with her. She said yes.

Leslie knew Ellen's family had experienced a rough year—Ellen's mother's illness, financial problems, and the mounting task of taking care of Ellen's needs.

> I asked her how she stayed so joyful, so optimistic when things around her were so tough. She continued to rock back and forth, tears now streaming down her cheeks. With her eyes scrunched shut, tears still squeezing out, she first pointed, then looked heavenward. She whispered, "Jesus." It rocked my world.[3]

As a parent, I want my children to have an unadulterated faith like Jacob's and Ellen's. I want them to sing loud, abandon their inhibitions, and fall headlong in love with Jesus, who embodies everything beautiful, who sings truth unashamed. I want them to whisper His name when life's circumstances are tough. I want them to value truth. I pray they don't exchange that glorious truth for empty lies. Through it all, I want my children to grasp the glory of obedience to Jesus regardless of what the world around them may say.

Part Two:

What Does Parenting Look Like in Today's World?

Building foundations and understanding the world we live in are both important, but how do we parent authentically in the midst of this shifting culture? How do we prepare our children to walk its dusty streets? What does parenting look like? In this section, we get down to practicalities.

Six

A Conversation

The Jewish faith has been characterized as
a "table spirituality" in which the central feasts and
holy days are celebrated around the altar
of the family table.

MARJORIE THOMPSON

We parent around the dinner table, where most of our children's joy and angst surface. Our practice over the last several months has been to play "high-low" every night with our children as we eat our dinner. Sometimes the table conversation buzzes with highs like when Aidan spoke fondly of his birthday party; other times, it sinks into lows as Sophie shares her difficult day. But through the ups and downs of childhood and parenting, we've come to realize that a conversational approach to life will best serve our children as they leave the home and venture out into a postmodern world. My friend Erin has experienced a similar phenomenon around the table: "We talk about salvation, death, genetics, the fruit of the Spirit, Amelia Earhart, sailing, Eskimos, friendship, loyalty…everything under the sun. I wouldn't trade that time for anything in the world!"[1]

The more we value conversation and discourse, the more we cultivate discussion in our home, the better equipped our children will be. Some have called this developing our children's "emotional intelligence," helping them to be able to interact in any situation. As we engage our children, we nurture this type of intelligence, where children learn instinctively how to think about the world and how to interact with the people in it.

Presence develops intimacy in our homes. Are we present enough to have conversations in the margins of life? Are we interruptible? Are we emotionally available? Patrick and I have grappled with these questions as we have sought to be conversational parents.

What Does Conversational Parenting Look Like?

Conversational parenting echoes Jesus' discipleship method. He walked to many villages with His disciples, practicing *peripatetic* spirituality. *Peripateo* is a common Greek word used widely in the New Testament with two primary meanings. One is to walk around, to circumvent, to walk, to go about. Jesus did a lot of this type of *peripateo* with His disciples. He walked on dusty paths. He ascended mountains with His followers. He ambled alongside them. He spent time. He was present. I find it fascinating that Jesus didn't start His formal ministry on earth until He had first been present, rubbing shoulders with mankind for 30 years.

The other meaning of *peripateo* is the manner in which someone conducts his life, the way he lives and behaves. The apostle Paul used this word a lot: "As a prisoner for the Lord, then, I urge you to *live* a life worthy of the calling you have received" (Ephesians 4:1). "Join with others in following my example, brothers, and take note of those who *live* according to the pattern I gave you" (Philippians 3:17). Being with our children as well as showing them by example how Jesus wants us to live is an important element of conversational parenting.

How we walk with our children, how we live our lives, communicates what Christianity is all about. *Peripateo* spirituality is reminiscent of Deuteronomy 6:6-7: "These commandments that I give you today are to be upon your hearts. Impress them on your children. Talk about them when you sit at home and when you walk along the road, when you lie down and when you get up." Wherever we go, whatever we do, we invite our children alongside us, sharing conversation and welcoming questions.

I'll admit I blow it often, particularly when I'm on a writing deadline and I can't seem to pull my head out of a story line. Last night Aidan told me how far he'd read in his latest book. I nodded but didn't engage him, didn't ask him what was happening in the plot right now. He walked away. Inside I knew I'd failed him, but I continued writing, preferring to wrangle with nouns and verbs instead of stopping and listening to our son.

Encouragement

One of the biggest fears parents face is that their children will rebel. In this current cultural climate, that fear has intensified. No surefire techniques are available to completely rebel-proof your children, but you can do some things to nurture a positive relationship with them. One is to determine to be encouraging.

I shudder to think of how many times I have not been kind or encouraging with my words. Yesterday morning, I came downstairs in a bad mood. I didn't take a deep breath when I saw Aidan's perfectly clean and folded clothes resting underneath his dirty ones in the laundry bin.

"How many times have I told you to PUT AWAY YOUR LAUNDRY BEFORE YOU THROW DIRTY CLOTHES IN?"

Aidan's eyes grew wide.

I should have held my tongue, but I didn't. I set it free, allowing it to release all sorts of frustrations unrelated to laundry. I laugh now when I think how comical I must have looked from Aidan's perspective. Before him stood his mommy with Medusa-like hair—I had just gotten up, mind you—yelling at him about practically everything. Even Patrick could hear me, two stories away. Note to self: This is not the proper way to encourage children!

We treat strangers amazingly well. We say please and thank you and prefer them over ourselves. But pull the veneer away from our homes, and what do you see? Backbiting. Harsh words. Accusations. Slander. Rudeness. Why do we treat strangers better than we treat our own families? Where has all the politeness gone?

We will endear our children to us if we simply take time out to build them up with our words rather than tear them down—or worse, if we fail to validate their feelings. Last night, Julia came in our bedroom, crying. "I don't want to go on my field trip," she said. "I'll stay at school."

"Why?" Patrick asked.

"Because you or Mommy won't go with me. I don't want to go without you."

I called her over to my desk, where I was sitting, and pulled her up on my lap.

"We can't go on that day, Julia. I'm so sorry." I tried to distract her by showing her all her pictures I had on my bulletin board. "Did you know that every time I see these, I smile?"

She shook her head. Still upset.

I realized I couldn't use the distraction method of parenting in this situation. She needed to know I felt her pain, that I validated her feelings. "That's hard, not having your mommy and daddy come on a field trip."

"Yes," she whispered.

I picked up a pad of paper, grabbed a pen and wrote one sentence. "Julia is the most amazing and adorable girl." I handed it to her. "I want you to know that, okay?"

She smiled a faint smile and walked away, but not before grabbing a few pieces of my paper and scribbling something on them.

This morning she popped her blonde head into my darkened room.

"What do you need?" I asked.

"Nothing," she said, but I could hear a smile in her voice. On the floor I found two notes: One read, "I love you so much more than candy!!!!" The other: "And you R the best in the world. Thank you!"

Listening to my daughter, letting her vent, validating her feeling, and then encouraging her with a written note changed Julia's perspective. My taking the time to care and listen resulted in her going out of her way to bless me back with kind words.

Modeling

If you desire to see your children open up to you, you must first be willing to model openness. I've seen this dynamic at work in our home. When Patrick and I share our struggles, our children feel safe to share theirs. Obviously, you keep some things from children to protect their innocence. When we went through some difficult ministry situations, we shared on a superficial level to protect our children from having to shoulder something very heavy. But we pulled our eldest daughter aside and shared a bit more because she was able to process it better.

Byron and Lisa Borden, church planters in Portugal, model this type of authenticity.

> For better or for worse, we talk about just about everything in our family. Sometimes I have wondered if we are too open with our kids about our feelings or frustrations, but we have very rarely not let them in on the things we are processing. I do think we have been appropriate in how we share and with what amount of information, but this openness about ourselves has created the open atmosphere of conversation in the house.[2]

Grace and Forgiveness

Last night, I threw a hissy fit in Julia's scary-messy room. I yelled. Threatened. Growled even. Later I found her in bed. I snuggled up to her, my heart broken. "Julia," I said. "I shouldn't have yelled at you like that. Will you please forgive me?"

She nodded, sucking in tears. "Of course I do, Mommy. I love you."

Sweet relief washed over me. I failed. But God—and Julia—forgave me.

We shouldn't miss this truth: We will fail. We will not always be encouraging and nice with our children. We hear the verses about fathers not exasperating their children and silently mutter, "Yeah, but what about when my children exasperate me?"[3]

If you want to invite your children into conversation, you must ask for forgiveness when your words have caused a breach in relationship. Asking forgiveness of your children is one of the greatest gifts you give them.

- You demonstrate that even parents fail.
- You show that Jesus doesn't call us to be perfect, but to be honest and humble.
- You show your child that he or she is not the only one who makes mistakes.
- You become a model for your children to follow when they wrong someone.
- You reveal how a family makes it through heartache—through daring to admit failures and seeking God's forgiveness.
- You repair broken relationships.
- You build trust.

Asking forgiveness, even when it's painful, shows your child that you value him more than you value your rightness. It models Paul's words and reveals you are becoming more like Jesus as you parent:

> Do nothing out of selfish ambition or vain conceit, but in humility consider others better than yourselves. Each of you should look not only to your own interests, but also to the interests of others. Your attitude should be the same as that of Christ Jesus: Who, being in very nature God, did not consider equality with God something to be grasped, but made himself nothing, taking the very nature of a servant, being made in human likeness (Philippians 2:3-7).

Imagine what parenting would look like if we simply embraced humility as Jesus did, if we did nothing from vain ambition, if we considered our children as better than ourselves. Asking forgiveness sets us on that path of humility and servanthood. And those who are humble servants are people whose children will naturally want to engage. Look at Jesus—how He seemed to be a magnet for children—and seek to be more like Him. Read the Gospels and see how many times Jesus welcomed discourse, how many times people sought him out. Wouldn't we love to have our children seek us out in like manner?

Opening Doors to Your Children's Hearts

Conversational parenting helps us understand what is in our children's hearts. My friend Renee has seen this happen in her home as her family readies to move overseas. "The more we talk as a family about the realities that are ahead, the closer we get to gaining a true glimpse of the hearts of our children. We don't always see what we'd like, but we are often pleasantly surprised."[4]

We won't know what is in our children's hearts if we don't provide a safe environment for them to share. If a child feels intimidated, she won't talk. If she thinks she'll be ridiculed for her questions, she'll clam up. Providing a safe environment is key to welcoming heart-revealing discourse.

As I have spoken at retreats and conferences, I've noticed that authenticity breeds authenticity. In addition to creating a safe space to share within our families, modeling authenticity is imperative. The more we engage with our children, the more they'll be willing to risk and share their hearts with us. Consider your friendships. With whom are you most likely to share your deepest hurts? The perfect friend who never has problems and makes fun of you when you do? Or the Velveteen Rabbit type of *real* friend who weeps with you when you weep and shares her own struggles openly? If you are not willing to share bits and pieces of your heart in an age-appropriate manner with your children, you will be setting the stage for your children to run to others with their hearts.

Coaching

Conversational parenting is developed over the years. When children are younger, they need parents to be directive—in a parent as teacher, child as learner model—so that the conversation is parent heavy. But as each child matures, parents must move from teacher to coach, learning the excruciating art of letting children make their own mistakes. Parents speak less, listening more to their children's rationale, validating as they wrestle through a decision.

If we direct and instruct well, we will probably struggle to don our less-verbal coaching style during the teenage years. Most parents make the mistake of holding on too long to the directive model, preferring to make decisions for children long after their kids have outgrown the need for it. We forget the importance of allowing life to begin to teach our children lessons.

"There is a difference between telling kids about life and saving them the trouble, and letting them actually experience life," Brandy Prince of Life Purpose Coaching said.[5] How do parents do that? How can we abandon the teaching hat for the coach's whistle? And what exactly does it mean to coach our children when they hit the teen years? We'll talk about this aspect of conversational parenting more thoroughly in chapter 10.

Byron and Lisa Borden have coached their children as they have dealt with living in Portugal, where the drinking age is loosely fixed at 16. "We don't know anyone who doesn't drink," Lisa said. Her children are often out with friends who have wine with dinner.

> So I chose to explain to them "how to drink." I told them that wine on an empty stomach will go straight to their heads, so go very slowly with the wine and bread they bring to the table before the food comes. I told them wine compliments the taste of the food and should be taken slowly or sipped. I felt that in so doing, I taught my kids how to handle alcohol appropriately in the culture around them. There *are* young people who drink just to get drunk here, just like everywhere else, and I was clear that I was not condoning that kind of drinking.[6]

She recounts how an American youth leader was surprised at Portugal's lower drinking age and asked how the Bordens handled it. Lisa shared what she said above. The youth leader said, "If all parents would teach their kids just that much, they would avoid all kinds of problems with alcohol!"

One Size Does Not Fit All

The beauty of conversational parenting is that it fits each child perfectly. When we talk about discipline issues with our children, we can tailor our words to fit each child. With Sophie, we use logic. "If you don't clean your room, you won't be able to see your friends this week." With Aidan, money matters. "We will deduct money from your checking account if your room is not cleaned." With Julia, incentives are effective. "When you finish cleaning your room, you may go out and ride your bicycle."

Of course life and conversation are never so cut-and-dried, nor should parents merely talk about discipline issues. "Our parenting is less about rules," my friend Shannon said. "We deal more with our older children on a case-by-case basis." She told me how she'd grown up in a highly structured environment while her husband grew up in a more permissive home. Together, they've developed a parenting style that blends the best of both upbringings. They listen to their children, validate their feelings, and mete out decisions based on several factors. One child may be able to go out at 17, but another may not, depending upon his maturity level.

Understanding your child's love language will enable you to better communicate more individually.[7] Sophie feels loved when she's touched, so I make it a point to touch her when I'm trying to chat with her. When we read together, we sit close, snuggled under a blanket. Aidan loves gifts. I am particularly sensitive to bringing him things back from a trip. When I do that, he is more apt to trust me relationally. Julia loves words of affirmation. She thrives when she's affirmed and is more apt to share more of her heart when she knows we value her unique abilities.

Purposefulness

Conversational parenting is both spontaneous and purposeful. Life and connection do happen in the margins of life, where little planning occurs, but being purposeful also helps communication immensely. Consider these two scenarios:

Scenario one: Mom picks her son up from school. She's distracted, thinking more about what she's making for dinner than how her son experienced school.

Son: "Hi, Mom."

Mom: "Hi. How was school?"

Son: "Fine."

Mom: "Really?"

Son: "Yeah."

Scenario two: Mom prays for son while he's at school because she remembers he's had a difficult test. On the way to pick him up, she thinks of good questions to draw him out.

Son: "Hi, Mom."

Mom: "Well, hello there. Should I give you a high-five, or do we need to drown your sorrows in ice cream?"

Son: "What do you mean?"

Mom: "Your test. How did you do?"

Son: "I'm not sure."

Mom: "How did you feel you did?"

Son: "Okay, I guess."

Mom: "Were you worried?"

Son: "No, I felt pretty good about it."

Mom: "I'm proud of you for studying so hard."

Son: "Thanks, Mom."

In the second interchange, the mom is able to know more about the son's day because she was purposeful in approaching him.

The word *purposeful* has many synonyms: *resolved, determined, deliberate, intentional, committed, decided, resolute, fixed, persistent, tenacious.* Antonyms include *unintentional* and *purposeless.* Look back over the ten synonyms and ask yourself the following questions.

- *Resolved.* How have I resolved to connect with my children this year? Have I changed the way I approach my children since last year? Why or why not?

- *Determined.* How have I been determined to really know my children's hearts in the last two weeks?

- *Deliberate.* What deliberate steps have I taken to reveal my heart to my children?

- *Intentional.* How have I been intentional with each of my children? How have I tailored my words to each child this week?

- *Committed.* Have I committed myself to knowing my children? How?

- *Decided.* What have I decided about each child that prevents me from connecting with him or her? What barriers have I erected? What obstacles have my children put between us?

- *Resolute.* How have I resolved this year to pursue the soul of each child? What prevents me from doing that?

- *Fixed.* Have I become so busy that I have not fixed my schedule to meet the needs of my children? Am I interruptible? Is my schedule too fixed? Do I fully fix my attention on my children when they are in the room?

- *Persistent.* When my children don't engage with me, am I persistent? Do I relate more to the woman or the judge in this story:

  > In a certain city there was a judge who did not fear God and did not respect man. There was a widow in that city, and she kept coming to him, saying, "Give me legal protection from my opponent." For a while he was unwilling; but afterward he said to himself, "Even though I do not fear God nor respect man, yet because this widow bothers me, I will give her legal protection, otherwise by continually coming she will wear me out" (Luke 18:2-5 NASB).

  This is an amazing parable for parents. May we be persistent, pestering our children with our knocking at the door of their hearts. But so often we are like the reluctant judge, bothered by the interruptions of our children.

- *Tenacious.* Are you a tenacious receiver and sender in the communication game? If a child blows you off, do you gather yourself and try again? How easily do you quit?

Purposeful communication happens when we dare to be tenacious parents who passionately pursue the soul of each child. The old adage applies to our communication with our children: They won't care how much we know until they know how much we care. Within the context of a loving, safe home where parents pursue their children in a variety of ways, communication flourishes.

Taking Time

Byron and Lisa Borden daily make a point to spend time with their children. For them, it's tea time.

> At four o'clock, our family stops for a cup of tea. We don't just each grab a cup and then go back to whatever individual thing we were doing. We sit down, usually on the front porch, and "be" together. It may end up only lasting 20 minutes before Byron has to get back to work or someone needs to get off to soccer practice—or it may last an hour. But this consistent space has done more than anything else to create an atmosphere of conversation in our home.[8]

Some families turn off the radio in the car and spend time talking on the way to school. Others turn off the TV and play games. Some curl up in bed and read stories before bedtime. In order to foster communication, families need to carve out small blocks of time to spend together.

Being Invitational

Conversational parenting invites chattering. The best way to foster communication is to become both a skilled asker and a patient listener. One night when we lived in France, I went into Julia's room to find chaos reigning there. Barbies were flung hither and yon like war casualties. Almost all her clothes were on crumpled display underfoot. Her bed was a mountain of toys. The next day I asked her about it.

"I was angry, Mommy. I wanted to run away."

Instead of probing further, I left it at that—until I helped clean her room and found her school backpack looking unusually plump. I opened it. Inside was a change of clothes, a blanket, a scarf, and pajamas. I showed it to Patrick.

We brought Julia close. "Why did you want to run away?" Patrick asked.

"Nobody likes me here," she said. She spoke of sibling rivalry, mean lunch ladies, an angry teacher. "I want to go away."

"Where would you go?" I asked.

"I was going to take the bus to Sophia Antipolis," she said. Our daughter Sophie takes the bus every day to Sophia Antipolis, where she attends an international school. It was the farthest place Julia could think of, I surmised.

"Where were you going to sleep?" I asked.

"Didn't you see my backpack?"

I nodded.

"That's why I packed a blanket. I'd use the blanket to keep warm."

Patrick and I spent a lot of time unpacking her emotions. We realized she didn't quite know how to express herself other than flinging toys and packing a bag for Sophia Antipolis. We reassured her that regardless of what she did or said, we would always love her. We let her know that when her sister or brother bothered her, she should come to us first. We told her we were so sorry that things at school were hard. At the end of our talk, when she realized we weren't scolding her, but inviting her, she ran to our arms, clinging to us tightly. Oh how we love that little girl!

Fifteen minutes later, Julia came downstairs. "Mommy, I want you to go look on your desk."

I went upstairs to my tiny nook office in our bedroom and looked on my desk. There, in the beautiful writing of my left-handed girl, was a sweet little love note. I wonder how different things would have been had we scolded her, grounded her, berated her for wanting to run away—if we gave into alarm and fear, letting our words fly without first listening. The more we asked questions, the more we learned about her fears and mounting stress at school.

Asking Questions and Seeking God

As parents we need to have an ear to the Spirit with an eye toward our children. We realize that we don't always know how to do this parenting thing. When our kids ask us questions like "Who did Cain marry if his was the only family on earth?" all we can do is seek help from God and be honest when we don't know all the answers.

Talking to our kids isn't always easy or safe. Opening up conversation means you'll take their doubts and fears along with their faith and courage.

A Balance of Grace and Truth

Jesus was the embodiment of grace and truth: "The Word became flesh and made his dwelling among us. We have seen his glory, the glory of the One and Only, who came from the Father, full of grace and truth...For the law was given through Moses; grace and truth came through Jesus Christ" (John 1:14,17). Conversational parenting thrives when we place grace on a pedestal in our homes. But the pedestal must be truth. It's a balancing act. If we have too much grace—if such a thing could ever be—our homes would reflect chaos as children did whatever they wanted whenever they wanted. If truth prevailed to the detriment of grace, we could end up with a handful of rebellious kids.

Our conversations must be speckled with both grace and truth.

Sophie and I chatted about a touchy subject one day in France. "Most people at my school hate America and think it's to blame for everything," she said.

"Why do you think they feel that way?"

"I don't know. I guess because we pollute the world and they don't like our president."

"Does America pollute the world?"

"I don't know," Sophie said.

"I'm sure America does pollute," I told her, "but it's not the only country that does." Here I snuck in a bit of truth.

"It makes me angry," she said.

"It's hard to hear people make fun of your country, isn't it?" I spoke words of grace to Sophie.

"Yes, very hard. I finally asked these kids the same question."

"What's that?"

"I asked them, 'When was the last time you've been to the United States?' That usually quiets them down a bit."

"I can imagine." Sophie and I mourned together after the conversation, grieving how much we missed the country so many made fun of. We experienced snippets of grace and truth—grace that it was okay to be sad and angry and bewildered, truth that people may be entitled to their opinions in a postmodern world, but that didn't necessarily make them true.

⁂

Having a conversational tone in our home beckons our children closer. It helps us know our children, what makes them sad, angry, elated. In a world that values discourse and debate, we do our children a great favor if we help them cultivate conversational skills. We love them well when we invite their thoughts. We model Jesus to them as we listen and empathize. My friends Jeanne and George Damoff emulate conversational parenting around the dinner table—the place where most of us connect with our children.

> We always ate dinner as a family and encouraged open discussion about any topic of interest. No one's opinion was mocked or ignored. No one's concerns were downplayed. We never hurried through dinner and often remained at the table long after the food had disappeared, especially as our kids got older. We laughed a lot together. We read the Bible and prayed together. We included guests at our table often, and the children participated in the conversation as much as the adults. They learned to express their opinions but also to listen to others.[9]

As we live our lives alongside our children, chatting along the way, they'll be better equipped to engage the world outside our door.

Seven

A Window

It is our children who serve as the doorway
we pass through to meet God face to face.

DAN ALLENDER

Developing a learner's posture is a positive tenet of postmodernity that has roots in Scripture. Jesus said the greatest disciples are servants. He applauds having a humble attitude—like the man who chose the low-positioned seat at the banquet. The longer we parents live, the more we realize we can't possibly know everything there is to know about life, God, family, childrearing. We are learners, as are our children. Viewed this way, our children become a window for us—a holy pane through which we can see God's activity in our own lives.

At its best, this journey of parenthood is an intricate dance. We waltz with our children when they are young, teaching them to dance to God's rhythm. But as a child nears adulthood, the parental waltz inevitably becomes a square dance, with children and parents laughing and whirling together to the rhythm of God's hoedown. Following our lead, our children eventually let go of our hands and discover the joy of dancing alongside us, doing do-si-dos around us. We'd rather control their steps as we waltz with our children, but God gently nudges us toward maturity so that we may let go of our grip and learn alongside our children.

What would our families look like if we could see our tween and teen children this way—as dance partners in a graceful choreography of knowing God? What if God wanted to use all the relationships in our lives, including those with our children, to bring us closer to Him? What would parenting look like if we became learners, dance partners, alongside our children?

Children: God's Sanctification for Parents

Children shape us. I long for patience as a mommy, only to see myself stumble, rail, berate, and become an impatient tyrant. One such day, I dared to look at my eldest daughter, Sophie, as she chased a toddler around the house in her new role as babysitter. The toddler stretched her patience thin, but she remained calm and sweet, continually reintroducing toys and songs to keep the diapered girl happy. I sat back and thanked God that He often teaches me more of Himself as I watch my children. I had only to look in my living room to see a superb example of patience that eludes me so often.

Jesus told us to welcome children. I've read the accounts of children scrambling onto His sacred lap, and I've prayed, *Lord help me to be a child welcomer like You. I don't want to grumble about those You say the kingdom of heaven belongs to.* As I travel further down this parenting road, I've realized Jesus' genius in this interchange is not merely to encourage me to welcome children or to humble myself as one. It is to dare to think children have more to teach me about the kingdom of God than I ever gave them credit for. Dan Allender agrees: "Our children raise us to the degree that we are willing to receive them as the gift God gave us to mature us to be like him."[1]

How does this happen? How do we allow children to become the window through which we see and experience God?

By valuing their intrinsic worth.

Jesus elevated children's worth as He beckoned them repeatedly in the Gospels. Consider this amazing link between welcoming the intrinsic worth of a child and our connection to God.

> At that time the disciples came to Jesus and asked, "Who is the greatest in the kingdom of heaven?" He called a little child and had him stand among them. And he said:

"I tell you the truth, unless you change and become like little children, you will never enter the kingdom of heaven. Therefore, whoever humbles himself like this child is the greatest in the kingdom of heaven. And whoever welcomes a little child like this in my name welcomes me" (Matthew 18:1-5).

Consider the phraseology here. Jesus asked a little child to "stand among them." The child didn't sit or bow. He stood—at Jesus' insistence—as if Jesus wanted the disciples to see the child on a face-to-face level. In a very real sense, Jesus said, "Look at this child I am putting in front of you. Learn from him." Today, He places our children among us. Do we value our children enough to see them as people who stand alongside us? Or do we dismiss them?

Jesus said we'll never enter the kingdom of heaven if we don't welcome children. Therefore, if we shun or dismiss our children or consider them insignificant, we miss out on God's blessings. But if we dare to not only welcome our children, seeing them eye-to-eye, but also to humble ourselves like children, our position in the kingdom of heaven greatens. Grasp that truth. Ponder it. If we dare stoop and bend our knee—watching our children as examples—great reward will be ours.

Jesus' next statement is even more astounding. When we accept and welcome our children, we are actually welcoming Jesus.

That's hard for me to internalize, particularly when I'm in the midst of reprimanding my children for once again neglecting to clean their rooms. Does welcoming them mean I stop disciplining? No. It means I value their intrinsic worth as I parent. And as I talk with my children, I search for clues that show me more of God. If I welcome them, I welcome the presence of Jesus in my life.

How are children windows to God's heart? And how can we as parents grow spiritually as a result of correctly reading our children and participating with God as we soul-nurture our families?

Jesus' Voice in Our Children

As I held Julia's hand on the way home from school, she lamented her day. "School is not heaven," she said. I agreed. This opened a door for me to talk about my fifth-grade year in school, a terrible year in which my teacher made fun of me for crying after my father's death and wrongly accused me of cheating. As we walked on in silence, I realized the depth of Julia's words. School is not heaven, to be sure, but neither is this life. God created in each of us a longing for a perfect place where tears would be stilled and grief abolished. Julia's simple words reminded me to live for that other place.

After our brief school-heaven discourse, she said, "Mommy, love hurts sometimes. Why is that?"

"Because when we love someone and they hurt, we hurt too. Like right now, I hurt because you are having a hard time at school."

"I love you," she said.

I squeezed her hand, thankful for her sweet gift of words. Love hurts, but she chooses to love me anyway. Like Jesus.

Children Help Us Slow Down

"Look at the leelee bug," Sophie told me one day when she was a toddler. She held a ladybug close to her face until it flew away on the breeze. Had it not been for her, I would have walked on by, forgetting the whimsy of ladybugs in flight and missing out on Sophie's sheer delight.

Children help us slow down.

Today I watched as my friend Samantha buckled her daughter Thea into her stroller. "I have to put her in the stroller when we're late taking Isaiah to school. Otherwise we take too long."

I smiled. I'd seen Samantha and Thea meandering home before, stroller-less. Thea flitted here and there, picking up rocks, talking to birds, singing songs. She's helped Samantha to slow down and see the beauty of God in the mundane.

I tried to do it all when I first had Sophie. I wanted to be able to cook and nurse at the same time. So I held her to my breast, my arm tired from the weight, and stirred pasta. Eventually, I realized this cooking method was not going to work. I sat down and nursed my baby, enjoying her, watching her. In that time, God gave me a much-needed rest.

Have you considered that children are God's tool to help you to rest? To slow down? Today, children seem to accelerate our lives. Driven by some sort of frenetic fear of not measuring up to the perfect parent, we traipse our kids to every sport practice or game, art event, after-school activity, and musical practice and performance. In this increasingly fast-paced society, we've listened to the lie that life is better lived in the fast lane.

Remember the old song that talks about slowing down, that we're moving too fast? That we're so hurried we don't let the morning last? Well, I haven't been feeling groovy lately. Haven't made the morning last. I have walked on cobblestones, though, and this is what I saw: Frode walking his three children to school.

I love how our Norwegian friend Frode walks his children to school. I run my children to school. Literally. We skip and run and walk very briskly because, well, that's what we do. We are hurried.

But Frode takes time. He talks to his kids. He meanders. He lingers. He is patient.

While I rush my children.

As I walked (briskly) home after seeing patient Frode, the Lord spoke to me about slowing down, about productivity, about my connectivity with Him.

"I want to slow down like Frode. I want to be less hurried when I walk my children to school. I want to cherish their childhood," I told the Lord.

With grace, I sensed God whisper, "You know, it's not how quickly you accomplish tasks in a day that matters to me. It's you I want. Whether you're slow or fast. Whether you get ten things or no things done. I love you. Period."

"Really? Could it really be that simple?"

"Yes, Mary, and here's the simplest part. Your day is not a to-do list. I don't look at the tally at the end of the day and either nod in approval or sneer in rebuke. I want to be connected to you."

I thought about that as I walked back home—at a much slower pace. God loves me not because I produce things but because I am.

I've often heard that message from the pulpit, but today it had more meaning coming from God's tender voice as I walked my children to school. It's as if my life had come to this pivotal point and I was quiet enough to hear the truth, almost as if for the first time.

Then I remembered the perfect parent list I coddled—the one with all the *shoulds*. If I don't do the *shoulds*, God will surely be disappointed. What God wants from me is simply being with Him, listening, talking, resting, abiding, interacting. And He often gives me gifts when I slow down to a child's pace and listen.

The degree that I stop and listen to His voice is the degree to which I will be free from my man-made list. I worry that I'm not befriending enough folks. I worry that I've isolated my heart from others. I worry that I don't interact enough. I wonder how to balance everything. I fret that I'm not enough for my children or my husband. But all God requires of me is to listen. To consider His short list (also known as His yoke, which is light) as more important (and probably carrying far more eternal weight) than my silly list. This is the key to unshackled freedom.

It all started with watching my friend Frode one day while walking my kids to school. But it ended with Jesus and freedom.

What a difference a less-hurried walk alongside my children makes.

Children Teach Us About Seeking and Finding

While I was cleaning the kitchen today, God reminded me about seeking and finding—maybe He wanted me to seek and find (and eliminate) the dirt lurking there. Jesus told many parables about lost items or people being found and what extravagant lengths folks go to when they've lost something of value. In our throwaway society, I realized how lazy we've become. If I lose something, I could either spend dedicated time looking for it, or I could replace it. This is where my mind went today as I searched for my pepper mill in vain. *Well, if I can't find it, I can at least buy another one.*

Children help us to keep seeking. I remember when Aidan lost Jolly, his stuffed dog. For weeks, he looked for it. The other children looked for it. We prayed that Jesus would help us find Aidan's faithful companion, but Jolly couldn't be found. Aidan didn't give up. And one day, stuffed behind closet junk, Aidan found Jolly—or perhaps Jolly found Aidan—and joyful reunion commenced. What had been lost was now found.

Adults tend to give up the hunt. Perhaps it would be worth our while to spend more time playing hide and seek with our children so we would be in the habit of searching and finding. The dogged pursuit of God merits the biggest spiritual blessings. Read the parables again about God's lost and found (Luke 15) in light of this. Do we really spend our time searching for God, or do we give up, settling for less than His presence?

Many parents have had the sickening feeling of losing a child in a store. I remember losing Julia once. She thought it would be great fun to hide from Mommy inside the circular clothes rack at a local discount store. I sent Aidan and Sophie looking for her as I frantically scanned the aisles. When I found her, she was laughing as if she'd pulled one over on me. I squeezed her until her laughing stopped. "Don't you ever do that again," I warned.

Seeking and finding is a lot like that. A frantic search. A relieved joy. The beauty in seeking and finding truths is that God, like in the story of the prodigal son, is seeking us. He waits on tiptoe at the end of the road for us to come to Him the same way a child waits with joy for a parent to come home from a long trip. That childlike anticipation, the beautiful seek-and-find aspect of God's character, is what He desires for us to possess.

The oft-quoted verse in Jeremiah 29 comes to mind. "'You will seek me and find me when you seek me with all your heart. I will be found by you,' declares the LORD" (Jeremiah 29:13-14). Watching our children and emulating them as they seek and find helps us to recapture childlike longing and hope. Aidan longed for Jolly. He wept for him. He hoped he'd find Jolly. So many of us have deadened hope, chastised longing. But longing and hope are necessary for spiritual growth. If we've lost hope, we've lost sight of God. The apostle Paul equated hope with the work of the Holy Spirit. "And hope does not disappoint us, because God has poured out his love into our hearts by the Holy Spirit, whom he has given us" (Romans 5:5).

Letting Go of Our Seriousness

I can't play. Or at least not very well. Growing up in a shattered home, I didn't have much opportunity to experience carefree play. Consequently, I have a hard time getting on the floor and interacting with my children through play and make-believe. I've had to face the sad fact that I'm not Mr. Rogers!

That's no excuse, I know. Play is vitally important in this shifting culture in which we live. Children, through the media and other peers, are being forced to grow up at a scary pace. They've lost the wonder of play.

Though I struggle to sit on the floor and look at Aidan's painted Frodo figurines, I realize how vitally important it is because it connects me to him. When we play, we confine ourselves to a small circle of community, ignoring the incessant "grow up" voices outside.

The more I dress a Barbie or read a book or jump rope, the more I capture something lost in my heart—carefree childlike joy. Ever try skipping down the road with a frown on your face? It doesn't work. I won't categorize all parents this way, but I can say that I take life far too seriously. God uses my children's play to stop my pressed-lip scowl in its tracks, trading it for smiles and laughter.

Adults embracing play is a lot like kids taking a bath. They never want to take one, but once they are in the tub, you can't coax them out until they're cold and wrinkled. I often shy away from play. Many times I fail in this area; many times my children beg me to play, but I don't. But once I jump into play, I never want to leave.

Children Help Us See God

I've been helping Aidan plan his tenth birthday party. He's nearly a decade, on the cusp between boyhood and manhood—a pivotal year.

And his desire to have friends over to celebrate this milestone is unbridled. He wants to talk about it every time he sees me.

"Mom, do you know who I am going to invite?"

I shrug, motioning that I have writing to do—about parenting, no less!

"Well," he continues, unabated, "Axel and Matthieu and Sam and…"

"Aidan, I'm working right now. Can we discuss this later?"

He shrugs and walks away, his enthusiasm squelched by my hard-heartedness.

I'm embarrassed to share this story with you. I feel ashamed. I understand what Jesus says about welcoming children, but instead of offering a welcome mat to my excited son, I threw a soggy towel at him. I missed out on sharing his enthusiasm, and I lost an important lesson Jesus might have been wanting to teach me. Aidan's joy over inviting lots of friends to his party eclipsed the actual party itself. Isn't that like Jesus? Heaven will be a party, to be sure, but His joy comes when He invites many, many, many people to it. But I would not listen to Aidan. And I didn't listen to the wooing message of Jesus, that He wanted me to give my life to welcome people.

Children Help Us Understand the Culture

"I want to be a meat catcher," Julia told me one day as we walked to her French elementary school.

"Really? What does that mean?"

"Well, I want to catch meat and then give it to poor people." What she said made perfect sense in her mind: Catch meat; feed hungry people. Postmoderns concern themselves with the world's plights—poverty, war, injustice, racism—and here was my seven-year-old reiterating the simple truth that poor people needed food and that she wanted to devote her life to meeting their needs. In our evangelical bubbles, we tend to err on the side of correct doctrine while neglecting correct actions. Children, however, seem to know God intentionally loves and cares for those in need. Paying attention to them, to their simple view of justice and kindness, serves as a window to God's heart.

Children Show Us the Father Heart of God

When my heart aches as my children struggle, I glimpse pieces of God's infinite love for me. I've come to appreciate the tenor of this verse: "As a father has compassion on his children, so the LORD has compassion on those who fear him" (Psalm 103:13). Because I had only glimpses of compassionate parenting growing up, I had a hard time understanding God's heart toward me. Only after having my own children and experiencing a deep maternal love have I more fully understood God's love for me.

Jesus said, "Which of you, if his son asks for bread, will give him a stone? Or if he asks for a fish, will give him a snake? If you, then, though you are evil, know how to give good gifts to your children, how much more will your Father in heaven give good gifts to those who ask him!" (Matthew 7:9-11). As we give good gifts to our children, we have the unique opportunity to grasp God's abundant and amazing provision for us.

Children Reflect Our Hearts

This ability of children to expose us is both fortunate and unfortunate. If you ever need to know how you are doing spiritually, watch your children. Pay attention to what they say. When I hear my children scold each other in a mocking tone, I can do one of two things. Reprimand them, or reprimand myself for setting such a poor example of grace (because they're flinging my words at each other).

The news isn't all bad, though. Our children catch our parenting just as a person catches cold. They're immersed in us, and eventually they may follow what we model. In my book *Building the Christian Family You Never Had,* I call this Inside Out Parenting.[2] What's inside us is what we tend to duplicate in our children.

By nature, I'm someone who wants to help my friends, particularly when they're having bad days. Sophie came home from school. "My friend isn't doing well," she said. "She's been really sick. I'm not sure when she'll come back to school." She shifted in her seat. "What do you think of throwing her a surprise party?"

"I think it's a great idea," I told her.

That Saturday, we threw Sophie's friend a surprise get-well-soon party, all by Sophie's initiation. It's something I would have done, the kind of thing she's seen me do. Seeing her imitate me in this way was a great encouragement that she is catching bits and pieces of Jesus in me. I am well aware that anything good that comes from me is His work in me, and any good in my children is His work in them.

Children Are Windows

Through our children, we see ourselves, where we are with Jesus. And we also capture snapshots of God as He works through our children. We see the beauty of this verse in Technicolor played out before us in our homes: "For we [parents and children alike] are God's workmanship, created in Christ Jesus to do good works, which God has prepared in advance for us to do" (Ephesians 2:10).

In this rush-rush culture that seems to shift daily, how can seeing our children as windows help us to navigate our world? As we stoop low to the ground to catch our children's eyes, we allow God to show and tell us His secrets. Jesus said, "I praise you, Father, Lord of heaven and earth, because you have hidden these things from the wise and learned, and revealed them to little children. Yes, Father, for this was your good pleasure" (Matthew 11:25). God's good pleasure is to reveal His secrets, His hidden things, to children. We will miss important truths from God's mouth if we turn the other way.

We live in a culture that devalues childhood but thinks itself infinitely wise. But a beautiful paradox should exist in our homes: Of all the communities in the world, we who value children will become the most wise. Childlike people hear God and can teach us the deeper things of God. Who better to train us to be childlike than the young people in our midst? What an opportunity! What a compelling way to live a countercultural life!

Remember, "God chose the foolish things of the world [who is more foolish than a child?] to shame the wise; God chose the weak things of the world [who is more helpless than a child?] to shame the strong. He chose the lowly things of this world and the despised things—and the things that are not—to nullify the things that are, so that no one may boast before him" (1 Corinthians 1:27-29). God uses children to show His strength. He establishes worship through them: "From the lips of children and infants you have ordained praise" (Psalm 8:2).

David said, "Behold, children are a gift of the LORD" (Psalm 127:3 NASB). They are gifts because God uses them in our lives to show us ourselves, teach us about Him, and bring us closer to Him. Wouldn't it be an interesting exercise to daily ask this question: How have my children helped me grow closer to Jesus today? What a change in perspective we might have.

The further we walk down the parenting path, the more we understand the multidimensional gift children are. God gives them to us for a short time. And we are the joyful recipients.

Eight

A Haven

*GOD's my island hideaway, keeps danger
far from the shore, throws garlands of
hosannas around my neck.*

PSALM 32:7 MSG

I remember running as a child. I ran everywhere. I tried to run away from fear. But as I ran into the safety of my home, I couldn't rest. Fear assaulted me afresh in the four walls of my home. I worried about my parents' drug use. I fretted about coming home to an empty house. I wondered if criminals were chasing me. I peeked out around our living-room drapes, worried I'd been followed. I didn't have a safe neighborhood, and the home that should have been a haven didn't shelter me from the world.

Perhaps because of that, I greatly value creating a haven for my children—a place where they can be free from fear, where their childhoods can flourish, where they can revel in the beauty and innocence of being children in a world that lures them to adulthood far too soon.

Postmodernity is knocking on the doors of our homes. It's out there. And some things it offers our children are good. Attention to the world's ecology. A view toward community. A hunger for justice. A heart for the poor and marginalized. And yet as parents loving our kids in a postmodern world, we still need to create a haven for our children, still need to protect them from the too-much-too-fast mentality of the world.

What is a haven? How do we create it? What makes our homes sacred spaces where we pursue our children's souls and connect them to us and to God? How can we foster a place for real childhood, where skinned knees and Popsicle-stained lips prevail over wearing adult stress like a heavy coat?

What Is a Haven?

Synonyms to *haven* shed some light: *refuge, safe harbor, sanctuary, shelter, sanctum, retreat, hideaway.* A haven is a place where children experience sanctuary, where they are sheltered from the harshness of life's storms. Our homes should be like a safe harbor from the roaring waves of this world. A home that is a haven is a place kids want to come home to and bring their friends. It's a place where they can be completely themselves with every emotion imaginable. It's a place where they know they are loved regardless of what they do or say. Marjorie Thompson, in her book *Family: The Forming Center,* adds to this definition of family as a shelter: "A healthy family is a shelter whose walls can offer needed protection from the more injurious values of the culture."[1]

How do we possibly create a haven where we protect our children from the snares of our current culture? Here are ten ways.

Let Kindness Reign

Consider this wise counsel: "Do not let kindness and truth leave you; bind them around your neck, write them on the tablet of your heart" (Proverbs 3:3 NASB). Parents forget that we must bind both kindness and truth to our parenting. If we only value truth, our children will wilt under our barrage of truth-filled words. Truth must be tempered with grace and kindness.

Christian parents desire that their children come to know Jesus. They long to see children repent and follow Him. If our homes aren't havens where kindness reigns, we place heavy burdens on our children, making repentance difficult for them. We forget these words by the apostle Paul: "Or do you show contempt for the riches of his kindness, tolerance and patience, not realizing that God's kindness leads you toward repentance?"(Romans 2:4). Kindness leads to repentance; harsh words don't.

How kind are you? Do you treat your children with the same sweetness you offer a stranger you are trying to impress? Have you forgotten the amazing kindness God demonstrates as He woos you to Himself? How quickly I forget about this. His kindness is one of the greatest motivators of my life, and yet I shell out shame and disappointment and judgment on my children, thinking these words will turn them around. Kind words make a haven. Kind words welcome repentance and relationship.

Welcome Hard Questions

All of us ask hard questions. But something happens when we become parents. Suddenly those same hard questions we've asked of God and others sound different coming from our children's mouths. But a haven home is a place where we welcome any and every question. We're not doing God a favor by ignoring our children's questions about Him, as if He needed us to protect Him! Let children question. Let them vent when they haven't seen a prayer answered. Allow them to chew on their perplexities. Create space for honesty.

Be careful about answering your children immediately with the answers you found through your own wrestling. Their faith must become their own. The wrestling is important. As you dialogue with your child through his theological ramblings, realize you are training him to engage in the postmodern world outside your doorstep. You are giving him a gift—the gift of discourse and discovery. This doesn't mean you never share your insights or opinions. As a parent, you are responsible to train your children. But don't jump in too quickly to solve problems. Pray through difficult questions, asking God to help you know the right time to engage and the right time to let your child think on his own.

We need to realize that children have the capacity to know God. They have a unique ability to see Him when we can't. Our job is not only to welcome questions but also to nurture a child's unique notions about God. Children uniquely interact with God, and this is something we should vigorously encourage and strive to learn from.

Be There

A haven is more of a haven when parents are around. Simply being there for your child creates a space of safety. I've struggled with this aspect of parenting, though. I deliberately chose to be a stay-at-home mother so I could interact with my children on a daily, purposeful basis. And yet I'm not always present. I don't always engage. I forget to look my children in the eyes and really listen.

Ross Campbell, in *How to Really Love Your Child*, emphasizes the importance of eye contact and physical touch. Both are necessary parts of being there for our children. He adds a third element, though: focused attention.

> Focused attention is giving a child full, undivided attention in such a way that he feels without doubt that he is completely loved. That he is valuable enough *in his own right* to warrant parents' undistracted watchfulness, appreciation, and uncompromising regard. In short, focused attention makes a child feel he is the most important person in the world in his parents' eyes.[2]

Oh, how I fail at this. It's hard for me to live focused on one thing at a time, let alone one child at a time. I'm prone to bouts of distraction. My mind is constantly flitting between several thoughts at once: *What will I make for dinner? I need to call the dentist. The floor is dirty. I have to work on the taxes today. It's time to take the kids to school. My feet are cold—again. The bathroom is growing things. The car needs gas. I should help Julia with her homework tonight. Don't forget the phone call at 3:00. Print off that handout before you forget.*

No wonder I have a hard time giving my children focused attention. I don't even allow myself that luxury! Though multitasking is helpful in the realm of household management, it's not life-giving to our children. I can't spend good, quality time with

Aidan while I'm computing taxes in my head. I can't concentrate on the nuances of Sophie's voice when I'm also checking my e-mail. I can't expect Julia to understand how to clean her room if I simply bark an order into the chaos.

I've seen this in play this week. I've nagged my children about their rooms (again!). I don't know why I continue this habit. It's not kind. It seldom gets the results I desire. So today I did something different. Before Julia left for school, I went in her room with her. I said, "Let's do this together, okay?" She smiled. We picked up her room together as I snatched eye contact here and there. I touched her. I encouraged her. Within five minutes the deed, which was once thought dastardly, became a sweet time of communion with my daughter because I chose to be with her in the moment, to favor coming alongside instead of barking an order.

Limit Media

I'm not against media. As I write this chapter, Sophie sits downstairs watching *Extreme Makeover: Home Edition*. It's a show that models our family's values—hard work, kindness, sacrifice, service. Something is redemptive about a show that takes a nearly ruined home and creates beauty from it.

But not all shows or movies or Internet sites replay those values. Jesus said this: "The thief comes only to steal and kill and destroy; I have come that they may have life, and have it to the full" (John 10:10). So much of our media is under control of the thief—Satan—who wants to steal our children's innocence, kill their sweet love for Jesus and destroy their minds. To create a home that is a haven, we must protect our children from media that has our children's destruction as its intent. We are doing them no favors by preparing them for a postmodern world if we allow them to know too early things like these:

- gratuitous or random violence
- hatred of people with differences
- sexual intimacy outside the context of marriage

- sexual perversion
- profanity, particularly the kind aimed at God

Our job as parents is to sift through media, to protect our children from growing up far too quickly. One movie may ruin innocence. One website might steal joy.

Jeanne and George Damoff dealt with media in their home by simply eliminating TV. In this, they established a home where child-like play flourished:

> By choice we didn't have a TV when our kids were little. Their heads weren't filled with images of immoral behavior portrayed as normal or, even worse, desirable. They didn't see advertisements telling them what they needed to be happy. They played outside, climbed trees, frolicked in the sprinkler, created cities out of blocks, made up their own plays and acted them out. They dressed in hand-me-down play clothes—not miniature versions of the latest teen fashions. We surrounded them with books—picture books, whimsical poetry, fairy tales. As much as it lay within our power, we kept them safe and gave them the freedom to soar on the wings of their imaginations.[3]

Simply limiting media will not protect our children from growing up too fast. We must not view parenting simply as doing everything we can to protect them. A time will come when our children will make their own choices. As they reach adolescence, we must make the shift from forbidding certain media to watching it alongside our children. Don, father of three teenage boys, makes it a point to discuss anything and everything with them, particularly as they watch movies together.

But parents shouldn't think that merely prohibition and discussion are sufficient. We should also be proactive, creating such an inviting and warm home that the negative things portrayed in the media have less lure. King David said this about God: "You prepare a table before me in the presence of my enemies. You anoint my head with oil; my cup overflows" (Psalm 23:5). David writes this verse to God the Father, the perfect Parent. God lavishes His love on us. We should lavish beauty and acceptance and joy and feasting on our children so that they will know that in the haven of family, their cups overflow. The more a family fills a child, the less he's apt to look elsewhere for fulfillment.

Play Outside

It's a shame our children can't roam about outside in abandon. Gone are the days when neighborhoods were incontrovertibly safe, where a child could ride his bike to the corner store without fear. How is it, then, that to create a haven for children, I'm encouraging kids to go outside? Because outside, children experience God. And so do we.

We create shelter in our families when we build in rituals that involve the outdoors. Camping, hiking, fishing, biking, walking, skating—all these activities connect us to each other and help us to experience God in a shared encounter. The more we regularly go outside, beyond the reach of cell phones, video games, computer viruses, and blaring televisions, the more we will experience genuine community in our families.

Weep and Rejoice

Romans 12:15 gives this sage advice to parents: "Rejoice with those who rejoice; mourn with those who mourn." Learning how to do this has been excruciating, especially when we were in France. To belly laugh when my children laugh has been easy, but entering into their grief has been much more difficult. Somehow I feel if I truly weep with my children and feel their pain, I'll have to look at myself and see what I've done to cause them pain. That type of introspection is never easy.

Watching our children adjust to French schools, Patrick and I had to deal with our children's grief and pain. But sometimes their pain was far too much. Julia couldn't easily express how hard school was or why she feared it. So instead of verbalizing it—so we could enter into it with her—she chose to take matters into her own hands. One morning before school we couldn't locate her. I could hear Patrick calling her name, issuing all sorts of ultimatums.

"Mary," he said. "Can you please come help me find Julia? I can't find her."

So I padded downstairs to Julia's room. Patrick uncovered her bed two or three times. He looked in her dirty-clothes bin—she is quite a small little thing and could probably fit there. "Julia, come out right now!" he said. I could hear panic in his voice.

It was Thursday. One of her dreaded weekdays. She attended school Monday, Tuesday, Thursday, and Friday in France. On Mondays and Fridays she came home for lunch for two hours along with Aidan. On Tuesdays and Thursdays she stayed at school during the lunch hour with the dreaded cafeteria ladies. At first she wept and wept every day before school; later she was down to Tuesday and Thursday, the days she was in school from 8:30 to 4:30. Hence the hiding.

I looked under her dresser. There's a smallish space under there where we once found her curled up, covered by a quilt. No go. Julia was nowhere.

Did she run away? Did someone break in and take our sweet blonde girl?

I looked up. There, perched on *top* of her armoire, sat Julia, like a blonde-headed gargoyle. Being the easily startled one, I jumped.

"I don't want to go to school today." Her voice sounded small. She hugged her knees.

We brought down our little gargoyle, thankful she was alive but worried about her ability to hide and scheme. How she got all the way up to the top of her furniture, I'll never quite know. I helped her get her clothes, sending her downstairs for breakfast. A few minutes later, off she went to school for the long day ahead.

Sometimes our children can't say what they feel. Sometimes they behave their feelings. I knew Julia was hurting, but not until I saw her perched like a gargoyle did I realize the depth of her grief. Julia gave me a gift that day—a snapshot into her heart. I had a choice then to brush it all aside and pretend her pain didn't matter. Instead, Patrick and I hugged her tighter, prayed with her, and entered into her pain with her.

That's what havens are for. To dress our children's hurts with bandages of attentive empathy. To celebrate our children's victories. To enter into their worlds, to walk around in their shoes, glossing over nothing.

Cherish Childhood

Yesterday Julia jumped rope over and over again. She created an obstacle course in the backyard with a bucket, a broom, some string, and a lot of ingenuity. She made us time her as she ran through her course. She was being a child, and we cherish that about her.

A few weeks ago, Sophie had her friends over. Though she's 13 now and her friends are teetering on the brink of adolescence with its trappings of boy-liking and hair-doing and make-upping, I loved hearing these words from one of the girl's mouths: "Hey, what do you want to play?" They played blind man's bluff for an hour in the backyard, squealing and laughing. Then they formed a circle and tied themselves into a giant teenaged knot. They included Julia and Aidan in their games. And I smiled. I love that my children aren't bent on becoming adults so fast. I love that my teenager continues to play.

Lisa and Byron Borden have placed a high value on childhood in their home. When their youngest daughter's school told them she could skip a grade, Lisa was flattered. But she thought and prayed about whether this would be best for her daughter.

> Yes, it would have felt good to say Heather was able to start first grade a year early, but we were more concerned about her losing that year of being a carefree child. We wanted to protect that last year of no homework, shorter school hours and more play and creative hours. It was a higher value to me that Heather learn to be creative and fill her play hours with imaginative games and even daydreams, than it was that she "get ahead" in the academics. We have not regretted this decision.[4]

Read

I am insecure as a parent. I worry I am messing things up. I don't always do the right thing. But one thing I do well is something so simple, you must try it if you haven't already. I read to my children.

Reading creates a haven because it gives families shared experiences. It opens up imagination. Good books teach lessons, not by preaching but by unveiling a well-told story. As we interact with a book together, more discussions surface. Camaraderie emerges.

Gladys Hunt, in her beautifully written book *Honey for a Child's Heart*, extols the virtues of reading together: "Reading aloud as a family has bound us together, as sharing an adventure always does…We have gone through emotional crises together as we felt anger, sadness, fear, gladness, and tenderness in the world of the book we were reading."[5]

Laurence Houseman echoes the importance of shared reading. "These family readings formed so satisfying a bond between older and younger that I can hardly think of family life without it; and I marvel when I hear of families in whose upbringing it has no place."[6] I agree. A home without books is like Junior without the Mints. Even when life is terribly hectic, we can slow its pace if we pick up a book and read together. Last night I read about Queen Esther with Sophie. Together we learned more about King Xerxes and how women were treated in the ancient world. Julia and I met Queen Jadis in C.S. Lewis' *The Magician's Nephew*. We laughed when Uncle Andrew's hat got pulled over his proud face. Aidan and Patrick encountered dragons and another world.

We also read the Book together, though to be honest, I don't think we read or interact with it enough as a family. One of the best things we've done is have the kids read portions of the Bible out loud. This helps them learn and pronounce difficult biblical vocabulary, but more importantly, in the course of reading, they voice their questions. Gladys Hunt asserts the Bible's importance:

> The Christian parent who uses both the Book and books has a distinct advantage. The Bible spells out precepts, the teaching of God's plan for man. It also tells us about real

people—their faith, their sins, their courage, their disbe-
lief—and we see the fruit of each in what follows in their
lives.[7]

Laugh Hard—but Not at Another's Expense

Laughter can be a salve to our children's hearts. It creates havens.
But it is a touchy thing.

One Valentine's Day, we gave each of our children a pink rose and
a Valentine's card. Julia came upstairs that morning. "Mommy, I love
you." She hugged me. "But Mommy?"

"Yes."

"Would it hurt your feelings if I gave my rose to someone today?"

"Not at all."

"I want to give it to Halvdan."

She trotted off to school, pink rose in hand, ready to give it to
Halvdan, a Norwegian boy in her class.

She came home upset.

"What's wrong?" I asked.

"Aidan's friend said he loved me, but it wasn't true."

"Oh, that's hard," I told her. "But you're only seven years old. Maybe
you shouldn't worry about who loves you and who doesn't. What about
Halvdan? Did he like the rose?"

She nodded, wiping tears. Apparently, she wanted *many* boys, not
merely Halvdan, to love her. Halvdan had loved the flower. He even
sent Julia a thank-you e-mail, complete with a photo taken of him
smiling next to his rose, now sitting in a vase.

"I'm in love with him," she told me. She sounded like a lovesick
17-year-old. I stifled a laugh.

"And he's in love with me."

This time, I couldn't help it. I belly laughed. So did Patrick. We
tried to hold it in, but we couldn't. "It's not funny," she cried. We apol-
ogized for laughing at her expense. We calmed her down. But when
she left, we laughed some more and vowed to pray and pray and pray
for our lovesick seven-year-old.

Laughter at someone's expense, as in this case, does not produce a haven. But a home full of genuine laughter at the funny things of life does.

Practice God's Presence

Brother Lawrence coined the phrase "practicing the presence of God."[8] It's something I aspire to, though admittedly, I fall short a lot. I admire Brother Lawrence, who found joy while doing the dishes or other everyday chores. I grimace at the toilets. Just now I asked Sophie to walk the younger two kids to school. She reluctantly agreed. "Can you do it with joy?" I asked.

"I could never do that," she said, her voice sullen.

I wonder if she said that because Patrick and I have failed to show her the joy of life with Jesus in the everydayness of life. How does doing this create a shelter for our families? Living joyfully in God's presence sets the atmosphere of our homes. Children will consider a home a haven if siblings and parents learn the fine art of reveling in God's presence.

We've recently found that Julia loves to do the dishes. Perhaps she's Sister Lawrence in training! She sings. She uses a special Julia-sized sponge while she spends time with Patrick. She begs to do dishes, particularly because she gets one-on-one time with Patrick. I wish I could always view the tedious tasks of life like that. To so much want to be in my Father's presence that I giggle and ask to do boring chores for the joy of spending time alongside God.

We are "to make the busy, boring, relentless daily life tasks the basis for...finding the presence of God."[9] His presence isn't always found in moments of breathtaking beauty or times of sheer joy. Our willingness to seek like a treasure God's presence in the menial often brings us deeper with Him. And the more we model that, the more our children will catch God's presence in the haven of our homes.

Creating a haven in our homes takes a lot of forethought and effort. But it's worth the time and energy. Home is the place our children return to, the compass they guide their lives by. As they leave our homes, they'll be more apt to return to what we value if home was a refuge. As the storms of postmodernism threaten to wash over them, a haven home welcomes them back. A house founded upon the Rock will withstand many storms because, ultimately, creating a haven is God's work. David said, "The LORD is my rock, my fortress and my deliverer; my God is my rock, in whom I take refuge. He is my shield and the horn of my salvation, my stronghold" (Psalm 18:2).

Nine

A Masterpiece

*Art is our memory of love. The most an artist
can do through their work is say, let me show
you what I have seen, what I have loved, and
perhaps you will see it and love it too.*

ANNIE BEVAN

Aidan, our highly artistic boy, came home from school one day,
weeping. It took a while for Patrick to coax words through sputter-
ing cries. "I did it wrong," he said, shaking his head. "My teacher said
I did it all wrong." He cried again.

"What did you do wrong?" Patrick asked.

"My art project," he said.

He showed Patrick his project as he sucked his breath in and out.
Together, they discovered what the teacher wanted. I was away on
writing business and called that night. Aidan told me the story again,
still crying.

"I want that piece of art she said wasn't right," I told him. "Can you
do me a favor and put it on my desk so when I get home, I can have
it? I want to hang it in my office."

He agreed.

When I got home, his creation—a swirl of pink, yellow, orange
and red lines and designs—welcomed me. It was beautiful. I couldn't
figure out why the teacher didn't think so. It hangs in my office, a
reminder that beauty and art are often in the eye of the beholder. It's

also a lesson to me to be alert and encouraging when I see my children's art.

Art Shows What's Inside

Art is a window to our soul. Perhaps that's why Aidan wept when his teacher criticized his piece. Perhaps that's why I cringe when I read a negative review of one of my books. A part of us bleeds into everything we create. For that reason alone, we as parents lose a great opportunity to know and love our children when we forget the importance of art in their development.

Erin, an artist, is incorporating art as she teaches her children about God. "Growing up, I didn't learn, really learn, about Jesus in Sunday school. My faith journey would have been so much richer if I had experienced the Bible as a child instead of being talked to." So now, she's building the tabernacle out of Play-Doh and sticks with her three girls. The only downfall is that her two-year-old broke off a piece of it! "If I had this experience as a kid, not just sitting in a chair, it would have been better. I'm learning so much more as a postmodern parent than I ever did as a child."

Gifts and Talents Are Avenues

An important part of parenting is determining each child's giftings. Have you ever considered that the particular way God wired your children is an avenue He's created for them to enter into fellowship with Him? Case in point: Aidan loves to sing. After spending a week at camp and learning new songs, we were heartened to hear him belt praise songs in the shower. He connects with God through song. The talents God has given all of us help us relate to the God of all creativity. So discovering your child's particular artistic bent and helping him see how that talent can be an avenue to Jesus is an important endeavor. Erin puts it this way: "The special things God has built into each of us were built into us for the purpose of His enjoyment and glory."[1]

Here are ten ways to bring art into your family.

Pursue SoulPerSuit

Erin is one of the engineers of a website called SoulPerSuit, an interactive art-based Bible study that merges scriptural truth with artistic response. When we were waiting for our church in France to get up and running, our family used several of the studies as our Sunday church. The results of integrating art, Jesus, and family have been beautiful.

The first project we did involved the lament psalms. We analyzed the structure of Psalm 12, a Davidic lament. The structure goes something like this:

1. An appeal to God, perhaps a why-is-this-happening-to-me question.

2. A description of the problem we find ourselves in.

3. A request to God ("Please help!").

4. God's answer to us in the midst of the pain.

5. Our words of trust and faith in the God who hears us.

Then, as a family, we wrote a lament together, based on our discussion of what we missed about our home church.

O Lord, we miss Lake Pointe Church
And all our Sunday school classes
We're left to watching services on DVD
In our pajamas
But it isn't the same, *pas de tout*
O Lord, build your church in France
So we're not so lonely
You have brought us new friends like:
Justus and Samantha
Xena and Laura and Merlin
Darina and Angelique
Melanie and Alexandra and Amber and Kenzie
Barney and Tiphanie

Daniel and Danielle
Oliver and Landry
And many more
We believe that you will build your church
And you will use us to do that here

After this, we each created small-scale art laments, showing not only what we missed about the United States but also how God had met us in our new home. Julia's piece showed a big house on one side and people on the other. "I miss my house in Texas," she said, "but God provided me with my family."

Aidan's art sported a plane over the top of his drawing with the words *travel* and *explore* at either end. "I miss my church, my home, and my friends, but I like the adventure of being in a new place."

Sophie's was most telling. She created a collage of everything and everyone she missed. "I miss my friends, our big house and big car, and Texas." In the midst of her collage was the word *life* hidden under a piece of vellum. I asked her what that meant. "Oh, that's easy. When we lived in Texas, life was blurry. But now here in France, life is clearer."

Had we not interacted with Scripture and art, I never would have known what resided in the hearts of my children at that point in our journey. If our desire as parents is to pursue the souls of our children, art is one way to discover that.

In like manner we've studied the book of Esther through a Soul-PerSuit study, creating Esther and Mordecai paper dolls. I taught the children how to create a Jesus-and-me art journal. On our first page we created a piece of multimedia art about our spiritual resolutions for the year. Julia drew her friends and said she wanted to pray for them. Aidan drew a line down the center of his journal. "I want wisdom to make right choices," he said as he displayed his art. On one side it showed what life was like when he made good choices; on the other, what it looked like when he made bad ones. I had no idea his desire was to gain wisdom, and to see him so clearly delineate wise and foolish living (as if his page were ripped from the headlines of

Proverbs itself) surprised and delighted me. Sophie made a collage with a watch, saying she wanted to give Jesus her time this year. Patrick and I also created our masterpieces, sharing our goals for the year. It became a time where we as a family could regroup around a common project and see into each other's hearts.

Take Art Field Trips

We also incorporate art into our lives by visiting museums and discussing what we see. One day, we had the privilege of seeing several museums in Florence, Italy. We happened upon the museum where Michaelangelo's *David* stood. Aidan, in his usual dry manner, said, "Daddy, why do they have to have so much private part art?" Before Patrick could answer, Aidan said, "I can't help it, Dad, I'm staring at it right now!" This, of course, lent itself to all sorts of parenting opportunities!

My friend Erin makes a fun game out of art museum expeditions. She devises scavenger hunts, asking her children to see who can find the most cats, fruit, circles, or rivers in the paintings that day.

Go Outside

Connecting with God's creativity, His art, means experiencing Him outside the walls of our homes. During my field orientation—a two-week intensive program designed to ready me for the European mission field—I learned the importance of nature. The facilitator taught our group about spiritual pathways—those ways we uniquely connect to God. Solitude, music, and study were some of the pathways he mentioned. He asked us to list the primary ways we connected with God. Though there were a dozen of us, nearly every one listed being in nature as his number one pathway to connect with God. And yet it is usually the first thing to go when families are under stress.

How do you help your children find our creative God in nature?

First, by helping children see God's big picture. Take them hiking, sledding, biking. I once took the kids to the mountains around our home in France so we could gather autumn leaves. We wound around the hillsides until we reached the top. For an hour, we clambered over rocks, took pictures, and filled our grocery sacks with colorful foliage. One Sunday, I announced we'd be taking a walk. We climbed the hill behind our home, venturing past some lovely villas, eventually ending in some woods. At dinner that night, we asked what the high of the day was, and every child said, "taking the walk." Helping children see God's big picture brings out their own creativity. Seeing God's night-sky star painting. Marveling at the snowcapped mountains He holds in the palm of His hand. Tasting ocean salt while sand grits toes.

Another way to help children understand God as the Great Artist is to study nature in micro. Erin studies a three-foot square of earth up close with her children. She encourages them to look for ant trails, tiny flowers, weeds, unusual insects. She asks questions and encourages her children to touch and interact with nature on a small scale. Teaching children to be observant as a spider weaves his masterpiece not only helps them with concentration but also gives them subjects for visual art pieces. After seeing the web, have children draw it. After discovering a new flower, ask children to paint it.

Being observant and helping your children become students of the outdoors can produce surprising results. Erin and her daughters realized a tree in her Dallas yard didn't drop its brown leaves. In the spring, her children noticed how the tiny green leaves were sheltered beneath the old brown ones. "We discovered that the tree uses the old leaves as insulation to keep the new growth protected during cold months."

Tell a Story

As a society, we've relegated story to the visual media where good stories last 20 minutes, one hour, or two hours. As a result of media saturation, we've lost the importance of reading and storytelling and imagining in our families. Jesus understood this powerful medium. Often to illustrate a scriptural truth, He'd tell a story. Parents should heed Jesus' example—to tell cautionary tales to their children rather than simply saying, "Don't do that."

Determine to bring great literature and poetry into the home. As you read together as a family, choose higher-level books that have captivating stories. Ask children to guess what happens next. By reading to children, you will be sowing a seed of longing in them. Aidan recently took off reading. Patrick started him on the Lord of the Rings trilogy. When Patrick didn't read as fast as Aidan wanted to know the story, he whizzed through it on his own.

Here are some other ways to bring in good writing: Read the Message translation of the Bible, which is more story based in its telling. Read old hymns and decipher their meaning. Pull out a few Shakespeare sonnets and encourage your children to try to write a rhyming couplet. Encourage storytelling around the dinner table. Praise your children when they bring their own homemade books to you.

Make Art Journals

One of the most rewarding things we've started as a family is creating personal devotional journals, using the medium of scrapbook art. A bit of background: In college, I was that girl who woke before dawn to spend an hour with Jesus. I memorized Scripture as I waited in line for lunch. I carved out "personal devotional time." When I got married and started having children, I battled tremendous guilt because I didn't do the super-Christian devotions as I had in the past. I felt like a failure and was sure God was mad at me.

For years, I questioned my devotion to Jesus because my time with Him tended to be sporadic and motivated by guilt instead of joy. I had forgotten the importance of this verse: "Each man should give what he has decided in his heart to give, not reluctantly or under compulsion, for God loves a cheerful giver" (2 Corinthians 9:7). Though this verse relates primarily to money, I've seen the wisdom in Paul's words as it applies to all of life. God wants us to delight in this life and to give to Him willingly and cheerfully. Viewing "devotions" as something to cross off my list or hit myself over the head with when I failed to do them robbed me of the joy of interacting with God.

So this year, I discovered a different way—one that fits me better—and I've taught it to my husband and children. As I read the Bible, I ask God to illuminate something to me. And then I respond—through art. I keep a three-by-five notebook. (The smaller, the better. It's less intimidating that way.) I journal in it through collages made of cut-out pieces of magazines, photos, newspapers, scrap paper—anything I can get my hands on. Doing this together with my children has brought a new level of intimacy. Patrick and I are better able to really see how our children are doing with Jesus, and we have fun doing it.

Attend Cultural Events

Our friends Michael and Renee told us fondly of a Turkish celebration they experienced with some exchange students they'd befriended. Going to an Indian restaurant with our friends from India opened our children's eyes to the world and its different foods. In France, we went to village celebrations. We once attended a mushroom festival where dogs were timed to see how long they took to find a truffle in a bed of straw. Keep your eyes and ears open for culturally broadening opportunities, particularly art, music, or food exhibitions.

Listen to Music

You can learn some amazing things about your family when you listen to music. It's interesting to me how we'll all respond differently to one CD, how each child will choose a unique favorite. Seeing that, and then asking him or her why, has proved to be an interesting exercise in our family.

When our family listens to U2's *All That You Can't Leave Behind*, for instance, God reminds me afresh of how very different we all are and how I can understand my children better.

My favorite cut is "Beautiful Day." It could be raining buckets on our car's windshield, but when that song comes on, I can't help but turn it up and look at the sky. How often I forget that each day is a beautiful gift, a gift to be cherished and reveled in. Every day is a beautiful day. How different my outlook would be if I enmeshed this truth into my life.

Patrick's favorite is "Walk On."

"I want you to play this at my funeral," he told me. I don't like talk like that, of course. It's a beautiful day, after all. The song speaks of going forward through pain, of letting go of things from the past and boldly doing what is right in the face of an uncertain future. I think it speaks to his sense of abandon, of his masculine craving for adventure—not only for adventure's sake, but for the sake of an adventurous life that counts.

Julia's favorite song is "Stuck in a Moment You Can't Get Out Of." Although only seven, she is an astute music critic. When the opening licks play, she says, "Mommy, turn it up. Puhhhlease!" When I see her in my rearview mirror, she is singing every complicated word.

Sometimes, like the song, she gets stuck in moments that she can't emotionally get out of. When she wants something and doesn't get it, she cries. In that moment, I resort to my trusty arsenal called "things that worked for the other children," trying to divert her attention. Of course, those ancient methods do not work. (Why don't they come up with a parenting model that fits *every* child? Why must I constantly come up with new methods? Sorry, I digress.) Unheeded, she stubbornly stays in her moment; she will not be swayed by mere words. So we battle, and I get stuck in moments of parenting that I can't get out of.

Aidan's favorite song is "New York." Yesterday Patrick and I were talking about Aidan. We decided that he is a city boy (much to my country-girl chagrin). He gains energy from walking city streets, peering up to tall buildings, and skipping to the sounds of the city. We gave him "Sim City" for Christmas, a computer game where you can design and plan your own city. He plays it every day. Although he could bring disasters like alien invasions or F-5 tornadoes to Aidanville, he chooses not to. I think something in his creations is sacred. Perhaps he doesn't want to rankle Aidanville's beautiful day.

Sophie knows all the words to "Elevation," which is amazing because it is a song of lyrical tongue-twisting. She likes the rhythm.

Along with Bono, I think she wants to live above life, elevated. She is also an elevator. She elevates others with her words. She encourages her brother and sister and is especially touched by those who face handicaps. One Sunday at church, a mentally handicapped girl who seemed to be her age kept turning around in her seat to look at Sophie. Sophie was patient and smiled at her. They exchanged drawings, and when the girl turned around again and offered her hand, Sophie held it for several minutes. Sophie elevates others above herself.

We seem to embody our favorite songs. Next time a song resonates with you or a family member, perhaps it's worth a deeper look. Use those preferences as a springboard to conversation.

Lisa Borden encourages her musical kids. "As I have raised my kids, I have desired to bless the arts in them. I do this by supporting their expressions in many ways from putting up with loud music, to listening to it with them, to engaging in discussion about music, to getting them to their gigs and back, even at dreadful hours of the night."

She tells the story of watching her then 14-year-old son playing guitar on the couch. "Trevor was playing something lovely. I was passing by behind him, and I paused and put my hand on his head. He tipped his head back and said, 'Whatcha doin', Mom?' I just said, 'I'm blessing the music in you.'"

Other ways to utilize music as you parent: Play classical music in the car and ask the kids what they think or feel as they listen to it. "What kind of movie is playing in your head as you hear this music?" Play music while you clean the house, preferably fast-paced music. Dance as you clean alongside your children. Make up songs as often as possible.

Cultivate an Open Mind

If we want our children to appreciate art, we'll need to let go of some inhibitions. Even if watching a ballet isn't something you'd normally enjoy, consider going anyway. At a worship arts conference in Geneva, I had the privilege of watching a ballerina perform to a worship song. It took my breath. I cried. I want my children to experience art in a similar way. But if they don't see an openness in Patrick or me, they may miss out on vital ways they can connect to God.

Ken Gire, author of *Windows of the Soul*, reminds us that "we reach for God in many ways, through our sculptures and our Scriptures. Through our pictures and our prayers. Through our writing and our worship. And through them, he reaches for us."[2] Having an open, childlike embrace of the arts actually welcomes bits and pieces of God into our families. Teaching our children to see art as a window both to God and to our soul that longs for God breeds a life full of expectancy and intrigue.

Lisa and Byron Borden actively promote keeping an open mind about art and God through 24/7 prayer rooms.[3]

> With paints and markers, clay, music and dance space, these prayer rooms have provided a private freedom for people to express themselves to God. The fact that we have hosted these over and over has modeled to our children that we value these alternative ways of communicating with God. Their expressions in paint, poetry or sound during those times have blessed me deeply.[4]

See Visual Art as Family Therapy

When we first moved to France, we had no furniture, no Internet, no TV. The children slept on the floor and wore the same tired clothes to French school day after day. Interestingly, all three kids embarked on creating PowerPoint presentations. They made collages about home, drew pictures, and added photos of their friends. They detailed their adventures—a form of therapy for them. It became the way they grieved a difficult move.

Watch Media with a Caveat

Our world is saturated with media. Soon a day will come (and sometimes I wonder if it's already arrived) where we will no longer be able to discern reality from fantasy. Therefore, we must not simply let our children engage the media blindly. Sit with your kids during a movie. Discuss special effects. Talk about the news around the dinner table. Pick apart a cartoon. Recently, Julia's been watching what I thought to be an innocent fairy cartoon, only to find out it was chock full of blatant occultic content—which was harder to discern at first since it was in French. This led to a brief discussion about evil and why we didn't want her to watch this show.

The Reversal: View Parenting as an Art

Michaelangelo said these compelling words about one of his statues: "I saw the angel in the marble and I carved until I set him free." Isn't this an apt metaphor for parenting? Less linear formulas. More art. Our children are God's creation. We receive them as chunks of unformed marble, and we are privileged to seek God, asking Him where we need to carve, shave, and chisel until their true selves can be set free.

We have the joy of partnering with our children in the act of creation. Just as Creator God breathed this world into existence, as His image-bearers we partner with Him and each other as we create. In this formation of a family in a postmodern world, where experiencing the arts has become more and more essential, we prepare our children to meet that world as we embrace the arts and creation.

Ten

A Coach

The Bible tells us that we are God's masterpieces
(poiema in Greek); not only creatures, but His
creations, His poems (Ephesians 2:10).
We are living epistles (2 Corinthians 3:3).
And so, our lives are meant to be listened to, because
it is God who is speaking into and out
of and through the symphony of the years,
and the masterpiece of a lifetime.

MICHAEL CARD

We are God's masterpieces, as Michael Card astutely said in the quote above. Seeing our children as amazing works of art with the handprints of God Almighty pressed into their souls helps us understand what a sacred job parents have. We are privileged to watch the masterpiece unfold, to revel in the unique brushstrokes of each child.

But what is the best way to reveal these works of art? How do we parent in such a way that shines the best light onto each unique child? Which parenting methods help us to enable our children to grow into their own skin?

In a word: coaching.

Coaching has spread through the Christian community like wildfire. It's the mentoring and discipleship of the millennium. In a postmodern world, where pat answers are shunned like chemically bathed produce, coaching has filled a significant void. What is coaching? And how can we implement it in our homes as we try to elicit the poetic uniqueness of each child?

What Is Coaching?

Coaching is different from showing or directing. A coach simply helps someone who wants to change to effect such a change. Instead of pointing out how a person needs to change, a coach listens to what the person wants to change. The person being coached is the initiator. The coach, then, helps the person latch onto a goal and develop steps or strategies to reach that goal. A coach is a cheerleader, but he does not do the hard work for the person being coached. He facilitates, listens, asks great questions, and places the responsibility for life change on the shoulders of the one being coached.

Placed in the context of parenting, coaching is a method we can use to help our children move from dependence to independence. Since coaching is primarily based on how each child wants to grow, it requires a shift in a parent's thinking. I no longer strongly suggest my daughter practice her violin. Instead, I ask my daughter what she wants to accomplish as a violinist, asking what steps she would like to take to get there and encouraging her as she tries to reach her goals.

Should I Coach My Toddlers?

Not necessarily. Though we do allow young children freedom to make decisions—you should see some of the clothing combinations my children wear—we need to be more directive when our children are young. Parents become coaches gradually through the years. The parenting pendulum swings from control to relinquishing control about the time the child becomes a teen. Very young children need and thrive in parameters. They need to learn to respect and be kind to their parents. Toddlerhood is a crucial time when a more directive parenting style is essential.

What Does It Look Like?

Coaching looks a lot like letting go. And that is hard. Most parents who get it right as directors and decision helpers have a hard time letting children make their own decisions and mistakes because being directive works. Tell a child to clean his room. He cleans it. Or, more realistically, tell a child to clean his room, nag, tell him again, take away a privilege, nag, punish, nag, and then he cleans it. Still, eventually, directive parenting works. Coaching looks like letting life teach children lessons rather than taking on that role yourself.

Brandy Prince, a certified life coach, gives the following example. Being an achiever herself, she struggled with not micromanaging both her sons' grades when they headed to high school. So she sat down with her eldest son and asked, "Where do you want to go to college?"

They spent some time on the Internet, pulling up different colleges and noting their entrance requirements. Based on that, her son Eric chose his high school classes. Instead of telling him he'd have to get certain grades, Brandy asked, "So what kind of grades will you need to have to get into these colleges you've chosen?" At that point, Eric could choose what grades he wanted based on his college choices. The GPA ball was in his court. Brandy also asked, "Of all these things you'd like to do to get good grades and do well on the SAT, what would you like to concentrate on first?" This, again, allowed Eric the freedom to choose the path he'd like to take—something that will greatly benefit him as he ventures out into the world.

When Eric got a few low test grades, instead of berating him, Brandy asked, "Well, what are you going to do about it?" She helped him come up with ideas to boost the grade on his own terms. By his own initiative, he approached his teacher and asked for ways he could raise his grades. Brandy cheered for him as he took ownership of his own goals.

Coaching is similar to the Love and Logic parenting program, where parents allow real-life consequences to teach children, empathizing when they fail and being available to children through the entire process of decision making.[1]

What Is Our Responsibility?

Letting our children make decisions, particularly ones that may harm them, feels counterintuitive, doesn't it? Our job is not to prevent pain, though deep down, that's what we'd prefer. As adults, we've already experienced our share of pain and heartache. Because we love our children so much, we want them to be spared.

Unfortunately, life doesn't work that way. We don't help our children when we eradicate pain. If that is our goal in parenting—to remove or prevent pain—we are setting our parenting goals far too low. Pain can actually be a good thing when viewed in terms of eternity and God's redemptive hand.

Take a quick inventory of your own spiritual life. When have you grown the most? When have you felt closest to Jesus? When things were peachy? Or when life threw trials your way? When our children experience pain, particularly when their choices have brought on that pain, they are better off if we don't rescue them. Remind yourself that the current pain is actually an amazing opportunity for growth in your child. If you control or step in, your child will miss out on important character-shaping opportunities.

Is It Letting Go Completely?

You may be wondering if I'm advocating a completely hands-off approach to parenting. May it never be! I was raised with very little parental input, and I'm still struggling with the consequences of that today. Part of viewing our children as masterpieces is understanding that even though you are not the sculptor, you do have a very close seat next to the Artist as He sculpts your child. Coaching means we let God do His work. We listen to our children. We provide a place for them to develop their God-given potential. We cheer for them when they struggle. We rejoice when they succeed. We laugh when they laugh.

Coaching is like teaching your child to ride a bike. At first you hold the bike, vowing to never let go. This is similar to parenting when your children are younger. Eventually, if the child is ever going to ride alone, you have to let go. But you don't run away. You run alongside, shouting encouragement. You can't prevent every fall. Nor would you want to because every fall teaches a child something. Still, you can be near enough to pick up a child when he does fall. You can believe in that child. You can provide a protective helmet and teach the rules of the road. Running alongside a child gives him a quiet confidence. He will believe that he can actually pedal a bike down a path without falling. Even if he does fall, he has a loving parent to console him. Eventually you pick up your own bike and follow.

Someday, he'll pedal off to college and start his own life. In the meantime, it's better that we let go of the bike but stay close. Others have said that we shouldn't prepare the road for the child, but prepare our children to ride the road.

What Does That Mean Practically?

Here are four things you can do as you coach your children and ride with them:

Remind your children of their goals. After a long period of asking great questions, after your child has come up with some reachable goals, remind your child at strategic times. Sophie is learning the violin—something she initiated. Instead of nagging her to practice, I remind her in a kind tone of voice of her goal to play well. Then the issue is hers, not mine.

Ask good questions. When a child is trying to get better grades but is failing, ask good, open-ended questions. A favorite coaching question starts with the words, "What would it look like if…" In the grade arena, a parent could ask, "What would it look like if you set aside a little more time at night for studying?" These kinds of questions help a child determine his next steps; they help him think about how his actions today may affect his future.

Keep the goal in front of your child. Without nagging, keep your child's goal in the forefront. "I love that you want to become a better soccer player." This will motivate and remind a child of his goal.

Cheer for your child. The apostle Paul says this: "And over all these virtues put on love, which binds them all together in perfect unity" (Colossians 3:14). Cheering for your child is a form of love, a way to believe in her even when her confidence is waning. Remember that love believes all things.[2]

Why Isn't Coaching Instinctive?

Coaching doesn't always come naturally to us. To let our children make decisions, to ask good questions, to keep their goals in front of them, and to coach with encouragement—none of these are easy. To help our children see the connection between their choices and the future is hard for us. Why is this?

- Most parents haven't seen coaching modeled. We are used to assuming that all children will eventually rebel and that to parent simply means gritting our teeth and enduring.

- Some view parenting as an all-or-nothing strategy. I'm either directing my child in a hierarchical manner or I'm not doing anything.

- Many people tend to believe that the more a child is stretching her wings, the more a parent must control and direct her, even though this strategy seldom works (unless you have an extremely compliant child).

- Coaching goes against the current evangelical Christian parenting culture because it's less directive and more organic.

Leaning into coaching is difficult because it means relinquishing some control. Proverbs 22:6 says, "Train a child in the way he should go, and when he is old he will not turn from it." Parents read that verse with an internal monologue: *I will train my child in the way I think he should go.* But training or coaching means we will let go of what we want for our children, painful as that can be, and help them determine their own path, based on their own strengths, characteristics, hopes, and passions—things that God has woven into them from the womb.

Does My Children's Behavior Reflect on Me?

An erroneous thought strangles parents and prevents them from plunging into a coaching model. It's this: *My child's behavior is a reflection of me. If that is true, I must control him.* Oh, how I've stumbled in this. How I've believed it, particularly in the grocery store when my children displayed all their rebellious abilities in 3-D. If I truly believe someone else's behavior negatively or positively reflects on me, I will spend a lot of time and energy controlling that person.

Everyone is responsible for his or her own behavior. If my child behaves badly, that is his problem, not mine. Sure, I may be embarrassed. But it's not my issue. If I own it, I must control him. I've been humbled to see this in my own life. My need to control and to look like the perfect parent is sometimes more important than my children! I'd rather control them so I come off as a passable parent than do the hard work of letting them fail and teaching them about the importance of their own choices.

Ken McDuff, an associate pastor of family ministries in California, touches on this. He believes parents have fallen into the trap of parenting out of selfishness. In other words, their goal is to get their children to behave.

> In practice, a parent-centered philosophy translates too easily into parenting goals conceived out of selfishness. Though parents (including me) don't like to admit it, we often have hidden motives behind our parenting tactics. We want to look good to our friends; we want to be unbothered by our child's activity. So, we require our children to behave in certain ways—not for their benefit, but for ours.[3]

I wonder how much my parenting is based on my need for control for the sake of my own selfishness.

The Message Behind Lectures

Brandy, the life coach I mentioned earlier, has come to realize an important truth as she's parented her two teenage boys. She's a proponent of what she calls "extraordinary conversations"—conversations where she interacts with her boys on a deeper level because she refrains from lecturing. "I know now that I cannot say to my boys, 'I love you. I believe in you. I trust you,' and yet lecture them. Both are mutually exclusive." She advises parents to willingly pull themselves off the lecture circuit. If we want our children to truly believe we are coaching them, we must do this. Our words are important, yes, but our actions—lecturing, yelling—communicate far more.

Jeanne and George Damoff connect freedom with this type of trust.

> We gave our children freedom as they demonstrated the wisdom and maturity to handle it. Yes, it was hard to let go, but we did it in increments. Trust was theirs to lose. If they made foolish choices, they lost trust and, consequently, freedom. Our kids always seemed to understand the fairness of this arrangement. We also instilled in them a sense of the big picture. From birth we spoke of God's plan for their lives—a very real, solid future for which they were created and by which they would achieve their ultimate potential and satisfaction in life. By His grace, they understood the importance of keeping the goal (His "well done") always in sight, and it spared them from many youthful follies.[4]

The Battle for My Child

It comes down to a choice. Parents who are allowing God to shape their children into the masterpieces they are must understand the battle and who needs to win it. In our children's preschool and grade-school years, we battle for them. We protect them from the negative influence of media. We read great stories to them, hoping to show them how characters in those stories make wise choices. We hold them when they cry. We intervene when teachers are mean. But eventually, we need to wean ourselves from that role as they leave the nest and begin to make lives of their own. Parents who love their children have a hard time letting go of the battle armor. Most of us continue to believe it is up to us to win the battle for our children instead of equipping our children to win the battle themselves.

Understanding and Empathy

Eventually we have to let go of our children. God created Adam and Eve and let them go. He instructed them about all the good trees and the one naughty-making tree and gave them the grace of free will. They didn't choose correctly, but God still loved them, still encouraged them. And eventually, by an act of amazing love, He sent his Son to walk the dingy streets of earth so He could understand our lives. Jesus, then, becomes our perfect Coach who understands.

> Therefore, since we have a great high priest who has gone through the heavens, Jesus the Son of God, let us hold firmly to the faith we profess. For we do not have a high priest who is unable to sympathize with our weaknesses, but we have one who has been tempted in every way, as we are—yet was without sin. Let us then approach the throne of grace with confidence, so that we may receive mercy and find grace to help us in our time of need (Hebrews 4:14-16).

Because Jesus lived through our own heartache, He can come alongside us. He understands us. He sees us. His model is our model. To endear ourselves to our children, we must walk a similar path of empathy. We must seek to understand our children's worlds by wearing their shoes. At the end of *To Kill a Mockingbird,* young Scout said this: "Atticus was right. One time he said you never really know a man until you stand in his shoes and walk around in them."[5] Jesus walked around in our shoes as we walk around in our children's shoes—so that we can understand them and be better coaches.

✑

Our children are masterpieces, created in the image of God,

entrusted to us for a time. How they move from childhood to adulthood depends on our parenting—a holy calling. We better prepare them to meet the world as we coach them to continually become God's masterpieces, helping them walk into a future that God has prepared for them.

Eleven

A Full Glass

Rivers of living water will brim and
spill out of the depths of anyone who believes
in me this way, just as the Scripture says.

JOHN 7:38 MSG

I've struggled with being a glass-half-full parent, always looking at the one cloud in the sky instead of the vast stretches of blue. Whether you're a pessimist—or realist, as I prefer to be called—or an optimist, you can enhance your parenting so you are authentically giving out of your soul's abundance rather than reacting in the moment. Many postmoderns value the cultivation of the inner life. This modeling of spiritual formation will not only help us become more positive parents but also give our children a tangible model that will follow them into adulthood.

Recently I heard these words: "I've had enough of running on empty."

My guess is that if I were to poll every reader of this book, each of us would admit to uttering or screaming these words, perhaps even in the past 24 hours. Ghandi said, "There is more to life than increasing its speed," but most of us live as if he told a lie. If we are to live gratitude-based lives with hearts full, we must again look at the unhurried life of Jesus, who didn't carry a cell phone or have a personal assistant or even a car! We must remember that to pour life into the souls of our children, our own souls must be filled up first. You simply can't pour life and encouragement into your children if you are empty.

I'm reminded of the analogy of the starving baker. From morning to night, the baker busied himself with baking bread to feed hungry villagers. He saw only the night sky as he traveled to and from work. But he never took time to eat. So enmeshed in his task of feeding others, he forgot to take care of himself, eventually starving to death.

The American dream lures us to be starving bakers, but our need isn't bread, it's deep connection with Jesus. We run around all our lives, never stopping for refreshment. We wonder why our kids are stressed, why they aren't passionate about Jesus Christ. Perhaps we have lost our connection with God in our busyness, and they are simply mimicking us. Of course, they are responsible for their own relationships with Jesus. Of course, God is sovereign and can fill them despite our weariness. But as parents, we set the tone for our home. Constantly flurrying shows our children that life is more about running, running, running than it is about slowing down enough to hear the still, quiet voice of God in the midst of life's chaos.

A friend recently pointed me to this quote:

> Quietness of soul, the fruit of truly seeking God, is seldom found in twentieth-century Christians. Far too many have come to accept turbulence of soul as the norm and have ceased to seek God with their whole hearts. Some have fled the cities to cloistered retreats in the hope of finding this quietness, only to discover their hearts still restless.[1]

So many times I settle for that place of rumbling turbulence, satisfied with hurry, addicted to rush. As I was writing this chapter, I received these words in an e-mail: "We seem to constantly be busy, yet I don't seem to get anything done."

What would our parenting look like if our glass were overflowing? If we had abundance to pour out on our children? If we followed the airline employees' instructions and pulled the life-giving oxygen mask on ourselves before we fixed it on our children's mouths? If we gave and yet were replenished? Jesus said, "If anyone is thirsty, let him come to me and drink. Whoever believes in me, as the Scripture has said, streams of living water will flow from within him" (John 7:37-38). When Jesus chatted with the woman at the well, He spoke of living water. He said that if she simply asked, He would gladly give her this overflowing water.

I remember singing the camp song "I've got a river of life flowing out of me." I performed the motions to the chorus: "Spring up, O well, within my soul. Spring up, O well, and make me whole. Spring up, O well, and give to me that life abundantly." But I didn't really understand what it all meant. My motions didn't match my parched heart. Today, sadly, it's much the same.

This chapter is about abundance and the lack of it. What does that have to do with parenting? Everything. Jesus wants me to parent from the abundance He provides, yet I often settle for less. Much less.

We are like the nation of Israel in Jeremiah's time. Jeremiah declared these astonishing words, words that rang true to an ancient culture as much as they do to our postmodern world: "My people have committed two sins: they have forsaken me, the spring of living water, and have dug their own cisterns, broken cisterns that cannot hold water" (Jeremiah 2:13). In this crazy, fast-paced culture, we have forsaken God by our busyness. Instead of running to the fountain of living water, we turn inward, digging our own bacteria-laden cisterns. We do a poor job of digging our own holes so that even the foul water inside flows out, leaving us empty.

Do you feel empty today? Incapable of walking this arduous parenting journey? So do I. I realize afresh that living in deprivation of soul is not God's intention for us. Let these words wash over you: "'I will satisfy the priests with abundance, and my people will be filled with my bounty,' declares the LORD" (Jeremiah 31:14). This is not merely a promise to Old Testament priests. In the New Testament, we are called priests. If you read further in Jeremiah 31, you'll see hints of this. God speaks of the New Covenant, of what was to come.

> "This is the covenant I will make with the house of Israel
> after that time," declares the LORD. "I will put my law

within their minds and write it on their hearts. I will be their God, and they will be my people. No longer will a man teach his neighbor, or a man his brother, saying 'Know the LORD,' because they will all know me, from the least of them to the greatest," declares the LORD (Jeremiah 31:33-34).

This was a foretaste of what we have the privilege of experiencing daily with the Lord—His constant, abiding, abundant presence in our hearts, woven into the DNA of our lives. Because of Jesus Christ, His death on the cross and His resurrection, we have access to the abundance of Jesus. We have God's laws indelibly written on our hearts. We have new life.

And yet as Jesus walked the earth, He saw haggard folks. He saw weariness in the eyes of many. As He looks on the earth today, I know He sees it. His words to us are the same as they were in ancient Palestine: "Come to me, all you who are weary and burdened, and I will give you rest. Take my yoke upon you and learn from me, for I am gentle and humble in heart, and you will find rest for your souls. For my yoke is easy and my burden is light" (Matthew 11:28–30). Let's unpack that verse a bit and mine what it has to say to parents in a postmodern world.

Come to Me

This is the only way to be a glass-overflowing parent. Either we dig cisterns, trying desperately to appear Jesus-like on the outside, or we come to Him and ask Him for His help so He can overflow our hearts with His living water. Jesus is the one who said, "I have told you this so that my joy may be in you and that your joy may be complete" (John 15:11). When we think of this chapter in the Bible, where Jesus portrays Himself as the vine and us as His branches, we mistake the imperatives. We sometimes confuse "bear fruit" with "abide." Jesus doesn't demand we bear fruit. He asks us instead to abide deeply in Him. Whenever I read, "Apart from me you can do nothing" (John 15:5), I worry. I wonder how many parenting miles I've logged by relying on myself.

All You Who Are Weary and Burdened

All of us have been weary and burdened. Most parents today carry weariness inside and out and are overburdened by schedules and stress and minivan meals. I have often found comfort in Paul's life because he seemed to understand being weary and burdened.

> We do not want you to be uninformed, brothers, about the hardships we suffered in the province of Asia. We were under great pressure, far beyond our ability to endure, so that we despaired even of life. Indeed, in our hearts we felt the sentence of death. *But this happened that we might not rely on ourselves but on God, who raises the dead* (2 Corinthians 1:8-9).

In Paul's eyes, the beauty of being overburdened is that we have the privilege of finally throwing in the towel and learning the art of relying exclusively on God's strength.

And I Will Give You Rest

Ah, rest. We all need it. But seldom do we experience it. Why? Because we don't come to Jesus. We don't realize He is the rest giver. We may try to manufacture it, but even in that, we forget He is the one who grants it. We take vacations that leave us weary at week's end, still in dire need of genuine rest. Perhaps the bigger question is this: Do you want your children to believe that following Jesus means getting burned out? That it means meetings and running around and stress? The way you approach life will rub off on your children more than your words to the contrary will. Do you want your children to have peace-filled, abundant lives? Then you must model that life by going to Jesus and asking Him for His rest.

Last year, God spoke this phrase to me: Joy in rest. For a year, I explored what that meant. I eventually came to the conclusion that we all rest differently. For my husband, rest might be an afternoon nap. For my son, it's painting models. I enjoy creating cards for people or taking walks in the neighborhood. To keep rest a priority, our family has set aside one day a week to unwind. We eat brunch together (something I prepare the night before), sing a few worship songs, read the Bible. We take walks. We put together puzzles. We go to our rooms and read books. In the cacophony of everyday life, we've needed this once-a-week plunge into quiet rest. As we've set aside time like this as a family, God has refreshed us. He promises He will meet us when we seek Him: "I will refresh the weary and satisfy the faint" (Jeremiah 31:25).

Take My Yoke upon You and Learn from Me

I'm an expert on putting my own yoke on myself. I'm so good at it, I don't even know how, really, to retrofit Jesus' yoke on my sore shoulders. This week, Patrick and I had an argument. I told him how he felt about me. I went on and on about how he must have been mad at me and how utterly terrible I was.

"Mary," he said. "I would never be that mean to you."

I realized then, perhaps for the first time, that I've been horribly mean to myself. I've assigned myself the task of shaming me. I go crazy with my overactive conscience, assigning things other people think about me that really only I think about me—bad things like what a terrible mother I am or how I'm an inconsistent spouse. I worry about every word I say. I am living in shame. All the time. My friend Hud says self-contempt masquerades itself as humility. I've spent a lifetime trying to appear humble, only to find that when I peel away the caustic layers, I find self-contempt.

One way to determine if you are making strides in humility is to ask yourself this question: How well do I receive a compliment or praise? It may seem counterintuitive, but the humble do not shy away from genuine praise. They are grateful for good words and don't excuse them away.

Self-contempt and minimizing other people's praise is not abundant, glass-overflowing living. I'm placing a tiresome shame-based yoke on myself that Jesus never intended for me. I am guilty of self-observing to the point of inflicting great amounts of damage to my soul. What yokes do you place on yourself? The need to be a perfect parent? The desire for achievement? A deep longing for parental approval? The fear of having to always be right? The debilitating worry that your children will stray? The need for control at any cost?

That's not Jesus' yoke even though we think it is. I have often thought I was being more holy when I accosted myself with words like these:

- You shouldn't have said that to her. You'll never tame your tongue.

- You should have done more to help that person. What kind of servant *are* you, anyway?

- Your children will need counseling when they're older. You're messing them up.

- You will never be an affectionate wife and mother. For the rest of your life, you'll fail in this area.

Even writing the words that populate my head is embarrassing. I have been extraordinarily mean to myself. I've treated others much better! And yet Jesus tells me His yoke isn't like the one I put on myself. It's different. His voice is not the berating, mean one. His is, as we will learn in the next point, gentle and humble.

Take His yoke upon you. Learn how to carry His light load, the load He puts on your shoulders. It's not up to you anymore. You don't even have to order your relationship with Him or determine exactly how you should grow. All you need to do is lay down your agenda, or in my case, my caustic self-killing words, and let Him take those burdens on His shoulders.

It's a learning process. Jesus calls us to become lifelong learners, always teachable, always attentive to His life-giving words. Isn't that what we want for our children in this shifting world? That they would become lifelong learners alongside us? That they'd be teachable and pliable?

It's our prerogative to take up His yoke first. We must demonstrate rest-filled living. As we dare to rest, our children will imitate us, promoting a legacy of rest for the next generations.

For I Am Gentle and Humble in Heart

If Jesus is humble and gentle and we are His followers, then we should also be humble and gentle. And if we are, then we will find abundance—a compelling paradox. The New American Standard Bible makes this correspondence between our humility and God's abundance: "The humble will inherit the land and will delight themselves in abundant prosperity" (Psalm 37:11).

I'm amazed at Jesus' gentleness—how He loved people living in the margins of life, how He stooped to come to earth to save us. I'm surprised at His humility, how He dared to leave the beauty and community of heaven to mingle with humanity. I'd always thought Jesus was somber as He exhibited these traits until I watched the Matthew version of *The Visual Bible*. It was the first time I saw a joyful, abundant, life-filled Jesus portrayed on the screen. It revolutionized my view of Jesus. He was not only a man with many sorrows. He laughed. He played. He joked. He is the ultimate representation of how God wanted humanity to be—filled with life.

And You Will Find Rest for Your Souls

What does soul rest look like? It's more than physical rest or emotional rest. It's peace that transcends understanding. It's knowing that God sees us. Even if our children rebel. Even if the world around us is chaotic. Even if circumstances outside of our control threaten to bankrupt us. Soul rest is that elusive beauty that beckons others. Have you ever wondered why Jesus was so attractive to people? Why He seemed to draw crowds to Himself? His soul was at perfect peace with His Father.

If we want our children to be attracted to Jesus in us, our soul peace is essential. Jesus said, "Peace I leave with you; my peace I give you. I do not give to you as the world gives. Do not let your hearts be troubled and do not be afraid" (John 14:27). Jesus is the Prince of Peace. He dispenses it in the same way He gives abundant living water to His followers. He did that for me one day as I ran through the hills of southern France. The day before, we found out the home we wanted to rent fell through, meaning we'd have to continue to live in our small home with a tiny yard. I thought living in a bigger home would make me content, fill me up. After all, it had gardens to rest in, a pool to play in. But on my run, the Lord reminded me that He is enough to provide those qualities for my soul. No swimming pool could do that. No beautiful garden. No large kitchen. Only Him. And He was enough.

For My Yoke Is Easy and My Burden Is Light

Everything in life feels so complicated. Life is not easy. Our load is not light. In a postmodern society, where our culture is shifting day by day, rarely are parents retrofitted with Jesus' yoke, daring to let go of the world's expectations—and even the expectations of other Christian parents—and letting God move them toward freedom. Jesus lifts our burdens and then gives us easier, bearable burdens—like loving God and loving others. We've made life so incredibly complicated, but it's really quite simple. Go to Jesus. Get right. Give Him your stress. Accept His gentle and kind leadership in your life. Modeling this way of living will benefit your children more than a thousand sermons they hear preached.

A Further Word About Abundance

Abundance is usually referred to in one of two ways in the Old Testament. First, abundance is something God possesses, like His abundant lovingkindness. Second, abundance relates to provision, like the abundant provision of food or a river's abundant supply of water.

In the New Testament, abundance is also found two ways—first in reference to Jesus and then to followers of Jesus. We are now the happy recipients of Jesus' abundance. It comes from Him to us through the Holy Spirit. "We all live off his generous bounty, gift after gift after gift" (John 1:16 MSG).

Still in Process

This whole idea of abundance has invaded my life lately. The Lord keeps whispering the word *abundance* in my ear. As I was writing this chapter, a clear example came to me, ripped from the headlines of the DeMuth Family Chronicles.

Patrick and I were required by our mission agency to spend a week at a leadership summit in Lisbon, Portugal. We didn't know what to do with our children during this time, so we sent out a request to our prayer supporters to see if anyone would be willing to fly out to France to watch our children. Cyndi e-mailed immediately, telling us she'd love to come out with her daughter Bethany and her friend Nancy. Since our kids knew these ladies and Bethany, it was a perfect fit—a wonderful answer to prayer.

We left knowing our children were in great hands. When we returned, they were very kind to sit down with us and encourage us.

"Your kids are so well-adjusted. We can tell you are good parents," Nancy said. Cyndi elaborated as well, pouring grace on us. We'd been worried about our children ever since we took them to France. Sometimes I could barely look at myself in the mirror because I felt so guilty about doing this to my children. But Nancy and Cyndi came from the outside and were able to objectively show us we were doing well as parents.

I should have rejoiced. That would have been the abundance response.

But I focused on one small comment, not even made to make me feel bad. Apparently during the week, Aidan had a hard time with his judo class (part of French PE). The ladies shared with me his struggle, how he had a hard time going, how one boy in particular was rough when he flipped Aidan.

Instead of taking these words as simply information, I went down the other path—killing myself with words of condemnation. *I should have known Aidan was having a hard time. I'm probably not loving him enough, not giving him enough of my attention. He confided in them because he probably felt he couldn't confide in me. I'm a terrible mother.*

This is not abundance!

Abundance is examining my heart, yes, but then letting go. And learning from what I experienced instead of berating myself with my inadequacies. The truth is, as a parent, I *am* inadequate. I disappoint my children, my spouse, myself. I'm helped in this journey by what my Scottish friend Nicole would call a "wee story" about a man who frequently walked past a monastery. He wondered what went on inside that holy place. He fantasized about his life inside the walls. Would he find unending bliss there? Would he be well fed? Would his problems fade like the setting sun? One day he gathered his courage and asked a priest who lived there, "What goes on in the monastery? Why are you so happy all the time?" Secretly, he wanted to know if he could become happy too.

The priest replied, "We fall down. We get up."

The villager shook his head, wondering what kind of secret this was. I wonder alongside him. Life is falling down and getting up. It's realizing that I can't always be an engaged parent. So often, I've been wallowing in the falling, forgetting the rising again. Isn't that the beauty of Christianity? That Jesus fell (died), and then He got up (was resurrected)? Isn't that the wonder of spring: what once appeared dead now springs to life?

This is not an easy practice for me. The dark thoughts about me not being attentive enough to Aidan swirl through my head, threatening to keep me down. I thank God that He is the God of the resurrection, that He can dust me off and set me back on my feet. I echo King David's words: "He lifted me out of the slimy pit, out of the mud and mire; he set my feet on a rock and gave me a firm place to stand. He put a new song in my mouth, a hymn of praise to our God. Many will see and fear and put their trust in the LORD" (Psalm 40:2-3). Abundance is God reaching down to parents and setting our feet on a firm foundation. It's God putting praise of Him in our mouths. The result? Our children, and the generation they impact, "will see and fear and put their trust in the LORD."

Resilience Is Key

I had the privilege of listening to my friend Hud McWilliams speak about resilience. He said it wasn't exactly like endurance, but more like our ability to spring back in the midst of trials.

I remember getting a job evaluation in college about this very thing. My employer said I needed to work on not letting the obstacles and griefs of life take over. That I needed to learn resilience. I'm not sure if I've learned it well, particularly when it comes to parenting. Life gets at me. Sideswipes me.

Hud's discussion then led to sharing our joy. I spoke up about my seeming inability to enter into the joy of having a dream come true, how I had a book release last week and I didn't celebrate because I was afraid I would seem stuck-up or self-absorbed. As I sat listening to the discussion that followed, the still, quiet voice of God struck me: *Do you trust Me with your joy?*

Selah. I had to pause and think about that one. Often God speaks to me more through puzzling questions than loud mandates. Why do I fear being joyful about a dream come true? Why have I often killed my own passions and longings because I was afraid of what others would think? Why have I stopped short of sharing my elation when my daughter Sophie helped her French friend come to Jesus?

Because of other people. I worry far too much about what they would think. If I rejoice, then I might appear stuck-up, or incite jealousy, or somehow appear separate from others.

This is the question we as parents should ask ourselves: Do I really believe God is big enough to handle my joy? Can I truly trust Him to shoulder the fear I have when I rejoice? Can I run to Him when others may misconstrue my elation?"

I've been living with the glass-half-empty Mary for far too long. It's become a security blanket to me, a way of living that smells of comfort. Perhaps faith and trust are more about taking a scary leap into joy than in glowering in depression. I don't want to live in that despair mentality anymore. I want to trust God with my joy.

I pray we all come to the place where we can say these words with conviction and joy: "Blessed is the man who does not condemn himself by what he approves" (Romans 14:22). To be free, to experience

and show God's abundance, to cease from condemning ourselves—
imagine how our parenting would change if we lived that way. Imagine how we'd touch our children's lives if we dared to live with that
type of joy.

Abundance and Parenting

What does abundance have to do with parenting in a postmodern world? I would venture to say abundance is the quality we possess—that God grants us—that our children need. If we can pass it
on through the DNA of our spiritual lives to our children, they will, in
turn, pass it on to an entirely new generation of folks dying for abundance. Postmoderns tend to live with pessimism. Imagine what this
world would be like if we all surrendered to that pessimism. Jesus said
we are to be salt and light to this tasteless and dark world. Learning
how to get up when we've fallen, with the strength God supplies, will
help us be the spice that entices, the candle that illuminates.

Twelve

An Authenticity

Don't you believe anything that woman says, Mara.
I'm sure your Nanny Lynn lady was a kind old
woman, but this one? I can see into people, I can. And
she is a fakery bakery. She cooks up lies, and makes
them look right pretty too—like frosting on a brick.

WATCHING THE TREE LIMBS, MARY DEMUTH

Robert grew up in a fakery-bakery home. From the outside, his family looked like a picture-perfect J.C. Penney catalog family. In public, they smiled. In private, Robert's dad yelled. And hit. Once he even broke one of Robert's bones in a fit of rage. Robert's father held a prominent position in a Christian institution. He had the respect of many, but his children knew the secret. They were privy to his antics behind closed doors. In one setting, his father would share Jesus and shepherd others; in another, he'd scream and shove.

His dad's hypocrisy made Robert want nothing to do with Christianity. Through the prayers and faithfulness of a good sports coach and the love of many Christian friends, Robert did eventually make his way back to Jesus. But first he had to reconcile the two faces of Christianity he'd experienced.

Ellen grew up in a similar home. Her father was a pastor. When the doors were shut to their home and their church clothes put away, all hell broke loose. As an adult, Ellen had her children dedicated in a different denomination. Though her family lived in the same town, barely two blocks away, they shunned her, not speaking to her for more than a year.

Today Ellen attempts to reconcile a kind Jesus with a harsh family. She saw hypocrisy firsthand and wants nothing to do with the church. She struggles in her relationship with God, preferring to run away from Him instead of dealing with the sticky issues of her past.

Mark grew up in a Christian home. He thought it was idyllic. Often he'd reflect on how loving and stable it was. Not until later did he realize most of his upbringing dealt in unreality. His parents merely went through the motions of church behavior. They obeyed because they were supposed to. They honestly believed that black people were a cursed race. They fueled their prejudice in many twisted ways.

Mark is walking with Jesus today, but he is taking a different path through a different church. His parents aren't happy with his choices and think he is going to hell.

Robert's, Ellen's, and Mark's families are sad representations of inauthentic homes. In every case, the hypocrisy of their parents turned them from following Jesus. Though some people from homes like these have struggled and kicked their way back into the arms of Jesus, many others are leaving faith behind, counting it irrelevant.

How can parents in a postmodern world positively influence children to embrace the gospel? For years, we've believed the lie that there is such a thing as a perfect Christian family. Entranced by a seemingly perfect appearance, parents have done their best to convey this plastic family to the world, regardless of whether or not it has represented reality. In the name of decorum and measuring up, we've done our children a terrible disservice. We've robbed them of the messiness that is the Christian life. We've prepared them for an unreal world, where sin and problems are hidden and accomplishments paraded. "Families often feel that their brokenness is unacceptable at church. They may try to cover their pain and sense of failure in order to project the image of the Christian family they think the church requires of them."[1]

I once knew a family who epitomized the quote above. They valued appearance, even to the point of saying that overweight people were always guilty of gluttony. Outwardly this family was thin, healthy, and beautiful, but behind their front door, their words and actions were ugly. The parents did what they thought was right in other people's eyes. Their children ate only healthy food. They practiced family devotions while their eldest scoffed. They evangelized people while threatening their children: "If so-and-so doesn't come to Christ because you were misbehaving, it'll be your fault." The children behaved in social situations, but once they were safe inside their home, they yelled and screamed at each other, following the example of their parents, who did the same. All of the children were angry. All of the children took their anger out on other children. They made fun of others. They mocked kids who didn't appear perfect on the outside. They puppeted what they saw their parents do behind closed doors.

It's a sad fact but true that kids will mimic the worst part of us. That makes me shudder, but even so, I've come to realize that hiding my warts will do little to help my children in the long run. Hiding produces shame. Shame sometimes prevents bad behavior in children, but it doesn't bring life or freedom or grace.

What are we teaching our families about Christianity? That it's a religion for perfect people? Didn't Jesus say, "It is not the healthy who need a doctor, but the sick. I have not come to call the righteous, but sinners" (Mark 2:17)? He said this after an interesting encounter. Jesus was teaching beside a lake. As He continued his journey, He saw Levi (Matthew) the tax collector and said the simple words, "Follow me." Levi invited Jesus over for dinner that night, and he invited a crowd of unsavory types, each authentic in his own way. Though they were needy, sinful, or deceitful, Jesus chose to hang out with them. He didn't preach a sermon, telling these folks to clean up their lives. Instead, He welcomed them, sharing the same food and table.

Those who appeared spiritually fit on the outside were bothered. They pestered Jesus' disciples, asking why Jesus would stoop so low to eat with these rubbishy people. That's when Jesus made His simple comment. He didn't come for the self-righteous. He came for the needy and broken.

This is the Jesus we follow. The Jesus who stooped. The Jesus who supped with sinners. The Jesus who commended the poor in spirit and chastised the proud. If we long to see our children follow that same Jesus, we need to take off our Christian costumes and show our real selves to our children. Why? Because they see through us anyway.

What is authenticity? It is one of the most heralded virtues for postmoderns. But before we delve into a discussion of what it is, let's discover together what it is not.

A License to Spew

"I'm being authentic," the spewer says to the spewee under the banner of authenticity. Hogwash! Yes, we are called to be honest with each other in our families, but that doesn't mean we say *everything*. Or that we use our words as weapons. The tongue, we must remember, is like a wild animal in need of taming. Consider these words from James 3:7-10:

> All kinds of animals, birds, reptiles and creatures of the sea are being tamed and have been tamed by man, but no man can tame the tongue. It is a restless evil, full of deadly poison. With the tongue we praise our Lord and Father, and with it we curse men, who have been made in God's likeness. Out of the same mouth come praise and cursing. My brothers, this should not be.

Whatever Pops into Your Mind

I remember going to a student leadership retreat in Canada. The thing that struck me about the speaker that week was this: She stood in front of us and fanned her Bible. Green ink peeked through everywhere. "What do you see?" she asked.

"Green," we responded.

She went on to admit her struggles with taming her tongue. Part of her taming included a quest for Bible verses related to this issue, highlighting those verses in green.

When particular thoughts spring into our heads, that doesn't give us license to share all of them with our children. Remember, Mary learned the art of treasuring things in her heart, and yet she was authentic. She knew when to keep things to herself and when to share. Parents have a similar mandate to guard what comes out of our mouths: "He who guards his mouth and his tongue keeps himself from calamity" (Proverbs 21:23).

Bringing this issue deeper, Jesus said that what we say reveals what's in our hearts.

> What comes out of a man is what makes him "unclean." For from within, out of men's hearts, come evil thoughts, sexual immorality, theft, murder, adultery, greed, malice, deceit, lewdness, envy, slander, arrogance and folly. All these evils come from inside and make a man "unclean" (Mark 7:20-23).

Sharing our words indiscriminately only reveals our waywardness with our children. Being silent and letting God heal from the inside out is much better. Jesus also said this to the outwardly focused Pharisees, who concerned themselves with appearances:

> Woe to you, teachers of the law and Pharisees, you hypocrites! You clean the outside of the cup and dish, but inside they are full of greed and self-indulgence. Blind Pharisee! First clean the inside of the cup and dish, and then the outside will also be clean (Matthew 23:25-26).

Boasting Our Strengths

Authenticity is not sharing how great we are, although those of us who have low self-images may need to learn how to share the positive aspects of ourselves. Inauthentic homes create and maintain image at any cost.

I call this image-parenting. With image-parenting, parents are more concerned with the family's perceived perfection in comparison to others than their shortcomings. An image-based parent is constantly comparing her parenting methods to others and justifying in her mind—and sometimes with her mouth—that her method is the best. She has not understood this verse: "For what makes you different from anyone else? What do you have that you did not receive? And if you did receive it, why do you boast as though you did not?" (1 Corinthians 4:7). Everything we have, every good quality we possess that we might be tempted to boast about, originated from God.

Paul gives good advice to image-based parents: "If anyone thinks he is something when he is nothing, he deceives himself. Each one should test his own actions. Then he can take pride in himself, without comparing himself to somebody else, for each one should carry his own load" (Galatians 6:3-5). Therefore, we need to let go of our own lofty parenting ideas or our own pride in our family when we are doing so only to show how much better we are than any other parents.

I've experienced this firsthand. I've had friends attend various parenting seminars. Because of the somewhat rigid methods, my friends came home determined to parent differently. All of a sudden, they looked down on me and the way I parented because my method didn't fit in with their prescribed regime. They'd use the positive behavior of their own children (while conveniently ignoring the negative behavior) to justify their proven methods. Tim Kimmel elaborates on this comparison phenomena:

> They [parents] often measure their effectiveness as parents by how they compare to others. They monitor other families and serve as a kind of "morals police," measuring these other parents' effectiveness by how well they meet their arbitrary and tighter standard. These parents have a knee jerk reaction: They are often quick to stand in judgment if some other set of parents falls short.[2]

In 2 Corinthians Paul tells us to boast, not in our strengths but in our weaknesses. My friend Sandi offers this advice to writers: "When you write, share your foibles while elevating other people's victories."

It's great advice to parents as well. What would this parenting arena look like if we honestly shared our defeats—with a view toward the beauty of God's redemption—and praised other parents who were doing well? What if we pulled away the curtain exposing the short Wizard of Oz of our families instead of projecting our own perfect family kingdom? What grace would infuse us all!

If we shed image-based parenting like a wool coat in summer, we'll be able to let go of the guilt and shame we hate to use. If we are constantly worried about our parental image or about how our children appear to others, we will use the twin "virtues" of guilt and shame to keep everyone, including ourselves, in line.

The future isn't pretty for those who boast in arrogance: "May the LORD cut off all flattering lips and every boastful tongue that says, 'We will triumph with our tongues; we own our lips—who is our master?'" (Psalm 12:3-4). Throughout the New Testament, we are told to boast in God, not in ourselves. We are to be humble enough to take the last seat at the banquet, letting God promote in His good timing. One question has resonated with me for years. It echoes through my heart when I'm tempted to be image-based: Am I living for my own reputation or the reputation of Jesus Christ? That's the filter we parents can use. The more we ask that question and heed it, the less image-based we'll be and the more authentic our homes will become.

Pretending to Be Authentic

I've met folks who understand that authenticity is one of the hallmarks of the Christian life. They've memorized verses like this one: "All of you, clothe yourself with humility toward one another, because, 'God opposes the proud but gives grace to the humble.' Humble yourselves, therefore, under God's mighty hand, that he may lift you up in due time" (1 Peter 5:5-6). They know sharing weakness is a hallmark of humility, so they do it. But they share in order to appear authentic, not because of a desire to truly be broken. One of the most interesting and convicting handouts I've seen came from author and speaker Nancy Leigh DeMoss. After reading her article, which listed the difference between broken people and proud people, I realized I've often acted authentic in order to look good, but I wasn't truly broken.[3]

⚬

I think we'd rather speak of wholeness than brokenness in the church today. Our lives seem to be bent toward some sort of ideal self that we are trying to achieve in our own strength. I'm surprised, though, when I look at the brokenness of Jesus—the one who was broken and spilled out for us. I realize that He uses broken folks like me and you to spread His love to a dying world.

This is one of the verses that defines me:

> Brothers, think of what you were when you were called. Not many of you were wise by human standards; not many were influential; not many were of noble birth. But God chose the foolish things of the world to shame the wise; God chose the weak things of the world to shame the strong. He chose the lowly things of this world and the despised things—and the things that are not—to nullify the things that are, so that no one may boast before him (1 Corinthians 1:26-29).

The Lord looked down on me from heaven. He saw me. I picture Him declaring, "I'm going to choose that girl down there. She's weak. She's broken. I'm doing it to bring Me glory. Her life will become one long boasting session for Me."

On the left side of DeMoss' proud and broken list, she cataloged the characteristics of proud people, on the right, broken people. I've rephrased some of them here:

- Proud people look at the failures of other people. Broken people are quite aware of their own failings and need for Jesus.

- Proud people must have control. Broken people eagerly surrender control.

- Proud people have demanding hearts. Broken people have giving hearts.

- Proud people ask to be served. Broken people willingly serve.

- Proud people blame others. Broken people can see when they are wrong.

- Proud people are defensive. Broken people are able to receive criticism with grace.

- Proud people worry about what others think. Broken people are concerned with what God knows.

- Proud people don't think they need to turn from sin, but are sure others do. Broken people live a life of repentance.

- Proud people need to be recognized. Broken people are eager for others to be applauded.

- Proud people want success. Broken people want others' success.

- Proud people are proud of how much they know. Broken people accept that they know very little and have a lot to learn.

- Proud people refrain from getting close to others. Broken people risk relationally, even when they may be hurt.

- Proud people find it hard to share their struggles with others. Broken people are authentic and real.

I read this list and realize how far I have to go, how often I slip into being a proud person, unyielding and hardened. Then I read the 1 Corinthians verses again and realize how very small and foolish I am and how very great our God is. Jesus set an example for us to follow.

He hung out with the lowly. He brushed up against broken people. He washed dirty feet. He obeyed His Father by dying on a bloody cross. He was crushed and broken for our sake.

We are more attractive to our children as we live broken, humble lives, not for the sake of our own reputations, but for the sheer joy of bumbling along as we follow Jesus. That kind of reality will infuse our children's lives in such a way that they'll be able to navigate the emerging culture.

So what exactly is authenticity?

WYSIWYG

That's the acronym for What You See Is What You Get. What is on the outside matches what's going on in your parental heart. Do you long to see your children's transparency? Is veiled hostility in your home, masked by dark silence? Your children are probably mimicking your hiding patterns. The more you can throw open the doors to your heart, letting the light shine into its crevasses, the more apt your children will be to welcome the light in their own lives.

Telling the Truth

So many of us fear telling the truth. I ached over writing the book *Building the Christian Family You Never Had.* Many times I wanted to put that book down, never to revisit it again. Why? Because in it, I shared the painful story of my upbringing. Trying to figure out what to leave in and what to take out was difficult. I knew, though, that I wanted to leave in enough so that a reader would understand I've been in the trenches of a dysfunctional family system. Thankfully, though I felt naked when the book released, my story—God's story, really—has helped others. That's the beauty of telling the truth about what's inside us.

When we do that, we endear ourselves to others. We show our children that being a Christian is not about working toward moral perfection, as if that could fully be realized on our earthbound pilgrimage.

Being a Christian is being a Jesus-follower—our gritty lives intersecting a holy God. If we bend toward trying to be perfect in our insufficient strength, we'll inevitably leave out Jesus. Kids will get the impression that to be a follower of Christ, we must become list-achievers, making a list of outer qualities and then, by sheer determination, accomplishing that list.

I experience far more closeness to my children when I admit my failures than when I trumpet my triumphs. A few days ago, Aidan was sick. In the night, I could hear him coughing. I was exhausted. Instead of nurturing him, giving him a drink of water and a tender touch, I prayed he'd miraculously get better. He didn't. He kept coughing. As he did, I tortured myself with words about what a terrible mother I was. In the morning, I almost couldn't look at Aidan, my shame was so great. Eventually I got over myself, sat next to him on the couch, stroked his hot head, and asked him to forgive me.

"I was trying so hard not to wake you up," he said.

My heart broke.

"It's my fault," I said. "I should have come to help you. Can you please forgive me?"

He did forgive, welcoming me into his ten-year-old boy embrace. Sometimes I think my children are far closer to Jesus than I am—they forgive so freely.

You may argue that sharing our foibles and sin with our children is counterintuitive. Won't it undermine our God-given authority? No. Consider the workplace for a moment. Would you enjoy working for a perfect boss who never failed, who succeeded at everything and expected perfection from you? Or would you prefer to work under a boss who sets realistic expectations, who shares her failures alongside her successes and strives to come alongside you in yours? Whom are you most attracted to? Shouldn't we parents be attractive and inviting to our children? Shouldn't we be the magnets that pull them toward Jesus? In this postmodern world, where inauthenticity is nearly a swear word, we must determine to share our hearts, warts and all.

King David, the man after God's heart, shared what was inside him. He spilled honesty and struggle into his psalms. "Surely I was sinful at birth, sinful from the time my mother conceived me. Surely you desire truth in the inner parts; you teach me wisdom in the inmost place" (Psalm 51:5-6). Over and over he pours out his heart before God and others. He disclosed much. He sinned much. And yet he loved God much. May we love God as much—in such an authentic, plucky way—so that our children crave to know a God so prone to forgive sinners such as us.

Novelist Lisa Samson demonstrates authenticity in her home. "It's utterly important. I blow it all the time. And I apologize when I do. I also don't think it's helpful if I never admit I'm wrong and I act like I never struggle. It would lead my kids to wonder why I would need Jesus. And yeah, I wouldn't be fooling anybody anyway, right?"[4]

Brokenness

The NLT translation of Matthew 5:3 says, "God blesses those who realize their need for him, for the Kingdom of Heaven is given to them." I once sat across from a woman at lunch. We were talking about Jesus. She had been in full-time ministry her entire adult life. She shared Jesus more times than I could count, and yet I couldn't believe the words she spoke to me. "I don't understand why Jesus died for me," she said.

I responded with something like, "Me neither. It's hard for me to wrap my mind around that."

"No, that's not what I mean. I understand why Jesus died for other people." She listed different types of sinners. "I'm not like those people. I don't really do much wrong. So I can't see why He had to die for me." I sat across from her stunned, without words. Here was a Christian leader who seemed to be parroting this Scripture:

> To some who were confident of their own righteousness and looked down on everybody else, Jesus told this parable: "Two men went up to the temple to pray, one a Pharisee and the other a tax collector. The Pharisee stood up and prayed about himself: 'God I thank you

that I am not like other men—robbers, evildoers, adulterers—or even like this tax collector. I fast twice a week and give a tenth of all I get.'

"But the tax collector stood at a distance. He would not even look up to heaven, but beat his breast and said, 'God have mercy on me, a sinner.'

"I tell you that this man, rather than the other, went home justified before God. For everyone who exalts himself will be humbled, and he who humbles himself will be exalted" (Luke 18:9-14).

I left our meeting saddened. She had not been broken but remained proud. And her children reflected her same attitude of pride and superiority.

The truth is, we are broken beings. To pretend otherwise is lying. We fear it. We run from it. We tell lies about our sufficiency. But that doesn't help our children at all, other than teaching them the "importance" of hiding. The beauty of authenticity is that our brokenness becomes a place where we meet God. Henri Nouwen says, "Our life is full of brokenness—broken relationships, broken promises, broken expectations. How can we live with that brokenness without becoming bitter and resentful except by returning again and again to God's faithful presence in our lives?"[5] Running to God in our brokenness and being honest about that journey with our children will directly benefit their relationship with God. Following God when we're perfect or our lives appear perfect is easy. Living a long obedience through suffering is much harder.

Jesus demonstrated that when He lived on earth. "Although he was a son, he learned obedience from what he suffered" (Hebrews 5:8). If we are to be authentic postmodern parents, we can't dismiss verses like that. God is more concerned with the state of our hearts than He is with our beautiful facade. And He often uses the vehicle of suffering to pull us to Himself, to teach us the weightier matters of faith, like humility and mercy and the power of brokenness. God doesn't call us to be perfect, but broken. That brokenness is a gift we offer our children—a gift they, in turn, will offer to a world seeking authentic spirituality. Author Marjorie Thompson agrees: "Others have aptly noted that the church has more than its share of latter-day Pharisees who are more concerned with the appearance of blameless moral behavior than with the weightier matters of mercy and authentic humility."[6]

Yes, authenticity is a hallmark of postmodern spirituality. But why is it beneficial to our souls and the souls of our children? Why bother?

Hiding Keeps Our Families in Darkness

> If we claim to have fellowship with him yet walk in the darkness, we lie and do not live by the truth. But if we walk in the light, as he is in the light, we have fellowship with one another, and the blood of Jesus, his Son, purifies us from all sin. If we claim to be without sin, we deceive ourselves and the truth is not in us. If we confess our sins, he is faithful and just and will forgive us our sins and purify us from all unrighteousness. If we claim we have not sinned, we make him out to be a liar and his word has no place in our lives (1 John 1:6-10).

I used to read these verses as if they were directed to me, an individual. If I confessed my sins, He would be faithful to forgive them. But look again. Count the times the words *we, our,* and *us* are used. Now count how many times the words *I* and *me* are used. Seventeen times communal words like *we* and *us* are used. *Me* and *I* are used zero times. These are communal verses, which means God intends us to live out our confessions in the context of community. And family is a microcosm of community. It's the first place our children are formed spiritually.

If we model hiding, we will not only walk in darkness but also promote that in our children's emerging spirituality. We can be authentic because of Jesus' great redemption. He has saved us and delivered us from darkness. Because of His work on the cross, we can be naked and unashamed. We can bear our souls to Him. By His grace and in His timing, we can bear our souls to our children. If we have trouble being authentic, if we prefer hiding to exposing, we need to reexamine our relationship with Christ. Before we knew Him, our tendency all the time was to hide. If we are hiding now, something is wrong with our relationship.

In the old song "Cat's in the Cradle," the father vows to be there for his child, but he turns out exactly like his own abandoning father, repeating the same patterns. The only way to change patterns is through a radical intersection of our hiding and Jesus' light, along with a healthy dose of confession in the context of community.

We knew a family once who were hiders. On the outside, the parents appeared to be lovely. But they embodied these verses:

> Everything they do is done for men to see: They make their phylacteries wide and the tassels on their garments long; they love the place of honor at banquets and the most important seats in the synagogues...You are like whitewashed tombs, which look beautiful on the outside but on the inside are full of dead men's bones and everything unclean. In the same way, on the outside you appear to people as righteous but on the inside you are full of hypocrisy and wickedness (Matthew 23:5-7,27-28).

When we got to know this family better, we found the decay underneath their appearance, as evidenced by the way their children acted toward others. They belittled. They made fun of friends. They coveted. They hoarded. They took.

Before I make it sound as if these people are terrible and I'm perfect, I need to stop. I realize how very fragile I am, how very prone I am to praise and wanting the approval of others. In that craving, I become pharisaical, preferring the darkness over showing Jesus and others what is really inside me. The most humbling moments of my life have come when my children exhibited the sin I was hiding.

As we raise children in this postmodern world, God uses our families to bring us closer to Himself, where all light resides. God will use our children and our faltering parenting journey to beckon us back to Him within the embrace of our little family community. I've been in darkness, and I've walked in light. I can say this: Dancing and laughter are more common in the light than in the darkness.

The Truth Helps Us Grow and Heal

Paul says, "Speaking the truth in love, we will in all things grow up into him who is the Head, that is, Christ" (Ephesians 4:15). As we learn to process the truth in front of our children—with God's leading—we will grow toward Jesus just as a sprout reaches for the sun. In our family community, the demonstration of growth will feed our children's souls. If we are willing to share our problems and sinful patterns, we instantly forge an accountability relationship with our children.

Patrick gets angry sometimes. He has a temper—not to say I don't, but mine doesn't manifest itself in the same way his does. Sophie has inherited his temper. As a parent, Patrick wants to grow in this area, and he longs to see Sophie grow as well. So he tells us when he's become too angry. He confesses his anger before the children. He asks forgiveness. We have been touched to see Sophie walk in his truthtelling, humble shoes. A few days ago, she raged and got in a funk. She went to her room for a while and eventually came upstairs to where Patrick and I were.

"Mommy, Daddy, I'm really sorry. I shouldn't have acted that way. Will you forgive me?" Her words echoed her father's. This is how being authentic can not only provide accountability for your own sins but also cause growth in your children. We could have preached sermons about apologizing for excessive anger, but Patrick's willingness to be vulnerable did more to change the dynamic of our family than mere words could have ever done.

Authenticity Improves Our Fellowship

When Patrick confesses his sin, he and the person he's confessed to immediately return to fellowship. Confession de-escalates strife. It puts a human face on our conflict. It restores relationship. Paul says we are members of one body, so we must tell the truth, even if doing so is difficult: "Therefore, laying aside falsehood, speak truth each one of you with his neighbor, for we are members of one another" (Ephesians 4:25 NASB).

Last week Patrick had a difficult day. His difficulty, and the silence that accompanied it, brought my day down as well. I asked him questions, but he couldn't articulate what was going on in his heart until much later. Once he was able to share his stress, we reconnected. I wonder how many families stay disconnected because they become so accustomed to hiding?

When I've let my anger burn toward my children without sharing it, I become cancerous, inflicting bitterness with my words and actions. I slam cupboard doors and whisper under my breath. This happened a few weeks ago. I felt as if Patrick and I were the only ones in the house making any effort whatsoever to keep it clean. I'd pick up after the children. Patrick would put things away that they should have put away. Eventually I exploded in a thousand mommy pieces at the dinner table. I would not recommend the manner in which I blew up, but after I shared my frustrations, I did regain fellowship—and a cleaner house to boot.

Families erupt in conflict. That's a given. Stuffing all our negative opinions and emotions down deep for the sake of harmony may seem preferable, but in the long run, it's more damaging. Best to get it out in a healthy way and restore fellowship. Romans 12:18 says, "If it is possible, as far as it depends on you, live at peace with everyone." As parents the onus is on us to do as much as we can, as far as it depends on us, to live in peace with our families. That doesn't mean we sweep angst under the carpet. To have peace, we must be willing to put up with a little authentic turmoil.

ꙮ

Authenticity is messy but necessary. We don't want our children growing up in homes like the ones I described at the beginning of this chapter. Hiding never helps. By God's grace, with His strength, may our families demonstrate how a frail family linked to a perfect God can be an enticing light to those longing for such community.

Thirteen

The Bible

When we use the Bible with children simply to teach doctrinal tenets, moral absolutes, tips for better living, or stories of heroes to be emulated, we stunt the spiritual formation of our children and deprive them of the valuable, spiritual story of God.

Ivy Beckwith

The Bible. It's the foundation of our lives because God, who created us, is its Author. Lately, I confess, I've felt a deep ambivalence toward God's Word, not because I don't enjoy reading it, but because many pastors seem to be preaching the same sermons over and over again. I'm weary of trite examples. I'm tired of 12 steps to improve my relationships. In our rush to exegete Scriptures and apply them to our lives, we can neuter the Bible's raw power.

Do we parents beckon our children to this sacred Book by our dissection of it? Or do we fluff it up, trying to make it appear pretty and easy? The Tower of Babel isn't pretty—it's full of confusion and shouting. Neither is Abraham's knife, poised above his son's pleading eyes. David having sex with Bathsheba and murdering to cover it up... well, we wouldn't let our kids read that in a novel! But the Bible has all these stories. We plop our children in front of DVDs that make Esther look like an *American Idol* contestant. We bring our children to Sunday schools where Noah's ark is painted in pastels. (I can guarantee there are no drowning, screaming souls painted outside the beige boat on a lavender sea). We've cowed to the culture of 30-second sound bites, making the Bible interactive, fast. And we've drained it of all its mystery.

How can we teach our children the Bible and adequately touch them with its depths? We start with a renewal of the way we look at the Bible, a reformation of our addiction to merely inductive methods. "If you see something beautiful, dissect it. Then you will know how it got so pretty. Of course, it'll be dead, but…well, at least you'll be smarter." So says Will Samson, husband of novelist Lisa Samson, commenting on his current graduate-level inductive Bible study course.

The Bible will change our lives as we grow in our knowledge of its wild and mysterious Author, as we embrace its tension and stop pulling from its sacred text our seven-point strategies for a positive life. The Bible is not man's way to get richer, stay healthier, or be better able to manipulate the Almighty as we dictate out-of-context promises. Some modern evangelical models of Bible study have stifled its tangible mystery. We've become surgeons, dissecting and cutting until we bring it to its lowest point of understanding. Ivy Beckwith, in her book *Postmodern Children's Ministry*, sums it up well: "The Bible was not created as the practical guide to the Christian life. It is not a self-help book. The Bible is a collection of ancient stories in which an ineffable, powerful and enigmatic God is the main character."[1]

What the Bible Is

The Bible is a gritty story inspired by the Holy Spirit. Though it has many authors, the message of God's redemption is woven beautifully through its pages. It is God's unique communication, in written form, to humankind. If we want to understand the mysterious God we serve, we must take in the breadth of the Bible, from prophetic books to books of the Law, from stories about Jesus on earth to the apocalypse, from poetry to cautionary tales.

The Bible is sometimes harsh. We do the Bible a disservice if we try to make it presentable to children as a compilation of moral stories with upstanding citizens populating its pages. It portrays human tragedy. It shares human debauchery. It's populated with people both heroic and flawed. The beauty of the Bible is its rawness, its revelation of a personal God who dares to intersect that rawness because of His great affection for people. Sentimentalizing the Bible with a flannelgraph depiction of its stories distorts our children's perspective of the grand story of God.

What the Bible Is Not

If you've been around Christian circles long enough, you may have heard the analogy that the Bible is like an owner's manual. If we simply go to the owner's manual every day, we'll know better how to live life and navigate relationships. Pastor Rob Bell has strong opinions about this shortsighted metaphor:

> Let's make a group decision to drop once and for all the Bible-as-owner's-manual metaphor. It's terrible. It really is. When was the last time you read the owner's manual for your toaster? Do you find it remotely inspiring or meaningful? You only refer to it when something's wrong with your toaster. You use it to fix the problem, and then you put it away.[2]

Neither is the Bible a self-help book. If we read it for the sake of gleaning easy steps to secure happiness and wealth, we've not only missed its overarching message but also forgotten how many times the Bible mentions that God loves the depressed and poor. I remember being sickened when I heard a preacher talk about Jesus wearing designer robes. He said that was why the Roman soldiers cast lots about His garments, that His robes were of the finest quality. But the Bible says Jesus had no place to lay His head, that He was acquainted with grief. I don't understand how, as thinking Christians, we can expect, by some miraculous hope, that we'll have lives of ease because of Jesus. If we call ourselves Christ-followers, we must be willing to follow in His steps. In the Gospels, I don't see Jesus becoming prosperous. And going to the cross certainly wasn't a health-conscious choice.

What Does That Mean for Our Families?

So what do we do? How do we reveal the mysteries of the Bible without dumbing down its extreme message? We simply tell the story and ask our children to respond.

> We can rob this story of its power by telling it badly, by sentimentalizing or sensationalizing or distorting it, or by analyzing or reducing it to a theological formula, or a lesson to be learned to please the teacher. We cannot rob it of its power by merely telling it too often. It deserves to be told—over and over again, directly as the Gospel and liturgy, and also as it is mirrored in fairy tale, myth, and other works of art. And our children deserve the opportunity to respond to this story, with clay, paint and crayons, with their bodies and their voices, with their imaginations and their hearts, in worship, in sacrament, in celebration, and in play.[3]

Godly Play

Troy and Heather Cady, church planters in Spain, use a method called Godly Play when they teach Sunday school. Godly Play Resources is a program developed by Dr. Jerome Berryman based on Montessori methods, applicable for any denomination. "It used to be we'd entertain in Sunday school, but when we used Godly Play, we found kids were mesmerized by it." Godly Play uses the vehicle of simple storytelling to help kids understand the narratives of the Bible. Godly Play's goal "is to teach children the art of using religious language—parable, sacred story, silence and liturgical action—to help them become more fully aware of the mystery of God's presence in their lives."[4]

When I saw Troy perform a Godly Play session, *I* was mesmerized. He rolled out a black cloth mat and spread out simple symbols in front of him. He picked up each object, sharing about its significance in the days of creation. He was teaching a mixed group, primarily of teenagers. You'd think they'd scoff at such a media-deprived presentation, but they stayed engaged as Troy told the story. Because the presentation was visual, I better remember the order of the days of creation. Because Troy didn't make conclusions about the lesson but rather allowed kids to ask questions, they became part of the story. When the story was completed, he invited the kids to touch the objects and then interact with the story through various play stations.

Troy and Heather say that Godly Play engages all levels of children, from very young to very old (me!). It doesn't neuter the story but shares it faithfully. It doesn't involve technology. The pieces used are handcrafted out of wood, providing a welcomed alternative to kids' extensive exposure to plastics and computer technology. It doesn't cater to a 30-second sound-bite culture. It's deliberate and quiet, and it validates the intelligence of the listener.

When my children and I studied Esther, we did something very similar to the Godly Play mode. We sat around our dining room table, heard the story, and then discussed it. From that, we created artwork based on what we read. The kids have kept their artwork. Every time they see it, they are reminded of the story of Esther. Many years ago, we did something similar to this using Joseph—of many-colored-coat fame. The kids remember that. We especially enjoyed Patrick's whimsical drawing of Joseph and his hippy striped coat.

Keep Your Humor

Teaching the Bible to children isn't easy. I remember my many, many attempts at trying to do family devotions. I was so freaked out that my children wouldn't know the Bible, or that we wouldn't fit the evangelical mold, that I subjected them to all sorts of strange experimentation. We tried setting aside one night as family night. We went through a prescribed curriculum, coloring in certain drawings, baking cookies for neighbors, memorizing the tiniest of Scriptures, complete with rewards. We sent our children to Christian scout-like groups where they had to memorize large portions of Scripture for badges and got points for bringing their neighborhood friends. We faithfully enrolled them in Sunday school. We played Christian songs in the car and listened to Christian novels on tape. I'm not saying any of these things were wrong. They all had their place, but I wonder how much of what we did was motivated by wonder and discovery and how much was motivated by guilt and the words *have to.*

I think we lost our humor in the midst of it all. In order to really engage our children with the Bible, we took ourselves far too seriously, like the author of this story, who describes her first attempt at starting a Sunday school class:

> I had hoped we could throw around a beach ball while we memorized a line of Scripture...But the kids had the attention span of fruit bats, and the boys would throw the ball too hard at one another, as if playing dodge ball... "God is love," I said through clenched teeth, and then threw the ball to a girl, who froze, so that it slapped her in the face like a whale's tail.[5]

Taming squirrelly children while trying to impart biblical truth can be quite humorous. We drain the joy of discovering the Bible for our children if we take its study so seriously that we forget to laugh and play.

Jesus Is the Central Figure

Jesus beckoned children. Not only that, they were attracted to Him. He was irresistible to them because He displayed the grace and beauty of God the Father with skin on. We do well to remember that the Bible's central theme is not a sentence about God's judgment. It's not even a paragraph about grace. Its central theme is a person. Jesus is the axis of the Bible. The Old Testament predicts His coming with great anticipation. The New Testament declares His story. If we were to view the Bible as a play, Jesus would be both the climax and denouement of the story.

We forget that. Some evangelicals have become so bibliocentric that they've become guilty of what I call bibliolatry. Patrick had the privilege of attending seminary. We met some amazing followers of Jesus while we were there. But we also met legalists, those who quote verbatim Jesus' words while being blind to the fact they were blatantly disobeying them in their homes. Once we had to help a wife go into hiding because her husband was hurting her. The husband, a seminary student at the time (he was asked to leave when this came to light), would call us and harass us at all hours of the night. During one such call, Patrick asked him, "What do you want to do when you get out of seminary?"

"I want to be a pastor."

"Well, don't you think," Patrick asked, "that you need to learn how to shepherd and love your wife first? Can't you see the discrepancy between you hurting your wife and yet wanting to help others?"

"My wife needs to learn to submit," he said, peppering his speech with expletive upon expletive.

Jesus has some interesting things to say to those who value God's words and yet disobey Him. If we want to teach our children the Bible, particularly in this postmodern world, where skepticism reigns and people smell inauthenticity a mile away, we must point our children to Jesus.

Jesus said this to the legalists of His day: "You diligently study the Scriptures because you think that by them you possess eternal life. These are the Scriptures that testify about me, yet you refuse to come to me to have life" (John 5:39-40). Jesus brings life. Obeying Him brings life. The Scriptures will become more alive to you and your children to the degree you stress the importance of following hard after Jesus.

The Beauty of Wrestling

We often approach the Bible with our children—and ourselves—trying to solve all its mysteries. When our children ask about God's Old Testament wrath upon entire nations, we pull out slick theological arguments so that God won't appear mean to them. Or we'll share, "That was the Old Testament. We are in a New Covenant relationship with Jesus now," as if God has changed magically between the Testaments. We don't welcome the wrestling. It makes us uncomfortable.

We'd rather have it all figured out, and if we teach our children our own pet theologies, we think we have adequately completed the task of bringing them up in the Lord.

What happens when they leave our home? When the world assaults them with contrary messages? Will our pat answers help them navigate this pluralistic society? Will they know how to answer for themselves the mysteries and perplexities of the Bible? Or will they crumble under the weight of someone else's argument?

I recently read an article about kids brought up under very authoritarian Christian parents. They were taught to respect their parents, always immediately obey, and be good citizens—all good things. But what happened when they became teenagers? What happened when they left home? Many rebelled because in childhood they were controlled, right down to the opinions they were supposed to have about Scripture. But even scarier, some kids raised in highly structured, controlling homes followed any sort of leader when they came out from underneath their parents—including cult leaders. They'd become so accustomed to looking to their parents for their opinions that they felt lost and afraid on their own, so they looked to the first authoritarian leader they could find to redefine themselves.

We've lost the beauty of wrestling. We've forgotten how to welcome it in our homes. Rob Bell applies the story of Jacob wrestling with God to our wrestling with Scripture. It's not an easy task. It's much easier to choose a set of beliefs and then defend them to the death, making sure our children mimic the proper tenets. We have a harder time saying, "You know what? I don't know why God took out entire generations of people. I could give you some theological explanations if you're interested, but to be honest, it rubs me the wrong way. I don't understand how a loving God could do that. I know He is just and righteous and can see everything, but it's hard for me to reconcile all that killing with Jesus." By saying that, we invite our children into our own wrestling, our own questions.

Unfortunately, we have reduced God and His Word to that which is manageable, nice, and agreeable. We've sanitized the Bible so that we don't have to grapple with its ambiguity. We don't want to be Jacob, wrestling hour upon hour with the living, breathing, wild God, only to walk the rest of our lives with a limp. It's messy. It doesn't perpetuate formulaic biblical interpretation like "If you do this, God will do these nice things. If you pull this spiritual lever, God will be forced to give you all the wealth you desire."

If we were really honest with ourselves, we'd admit that we do wrestle with the sticky issues of the Bible, but we don't often give ourselves permission to show that struggle. Instead of hiding what is inside or adopting everyone else's airtight explanations for the difficulties of the Bible, why not dialogue? Why not bring our concerns to the family table? Why not show our disappointment when God doesn't answer a prayer in the way we hoped? By doing this, we train children to recognize that asking questions is all right, that God's shoulders are big enough to hold our doubts. When our children leave home, they will leave knowing that the Bible is a difficult but life-filled book. Having wrestled with it and owned that wrestling, they'll be better equipped to handle it when others question their beliefs.

Our Brains Are Small

The reason I get weary of the Bible, as I mentioned earlier, is that I've heard thousands of sermons about it—so much so that the life has been leached from it. I now know all the "correct" interpretations of various passages. I know the Greek and Hebrew words. I've heard all the illustrations, pulled from sermon illustration books. All this has led me to have a rather myopic view of the Scriptures, stripped of its majesty like a lion shorn. But then I read the book of Job and everything changes. Why? Because I realize how very wee my brain is and how utterly "other" God is. How can I possibly know everything there is to know about the Bible? Isn't that an arrogant thing to think? How could I possibly navigate all its mysteries?

Job questioned God, and God responded by asking him questions like these:

- "Where were you when I laid the earth's foundation? Tell me if you understand."

- "Who shut up the sea behind doors when it burst forth from the womb?"

- "Have you ever given orders to the morning, or shown the dawn its place?"

- "Have the gates of death been shown to you? Have you seen the gates of the shadow of death?"

- "Can you bind the beautiful Pleiades? Can you loose the cords of Orion?"

- "Who endowed the heart with wisdom or gave understanding to the mind?"[6]

On and on God goes, asking Job impossible questions, questions no mere man could answer in a hundred lifetimes. Job was humbled by the sheer fact that God was big and he was not. This is how he responded to God's pages of questions: "Surely I spoke of things I did not understand, things too wonderful for me to know" (Job 42:3).

The Bible is mysterious because its Author is beyond our minds. John the Baptist summed it up well when he said of Jesus, "He has come from above and is greater than anyone else. I am of the earth, and my understanding is limited to the things of the earth, but he has come from heaven" (John 3:31 NLT). How can we fully explore the depths of God's Word when we are of this earth and our knowledge is finite?

Remember the Target

Patrick has a great illustration that is beneficial to adults and children alike. He draws a target on a whiteboard. In the middle he writes things like Jesus dying on the cross, the virgin birth, God as Creator, the Holy Spirit indwelling believers—the essentials of the historic Christian faith. Then he draws circles around the target. Toward the center, he might write views of women in ministry or alcohol consumption. On the outer rings he may scribble speaking in tongues or diet restrictions. Then he says, "the middle is what you would die for. If someone pointed a gun to your head and asked if you believed these core things, you would say yes and be willing to die for these. The farther away you go from the center toward the peripheral issues of the Christian faith, the less you'd be willing to die for that belief."

As we venture to the outer reaches of the circle, where head coverings for women or a glass of wine with dinner may lurk, we need to offer grace and charity to those who believe differently. Consider determining as a family what things you would be willing to die for. Consulting or even memorizing the creeds will give you a good idea of Christianity's essentials.

When our children leave home, they'll be confronted with all sorts of pet theologies as people pull nonessentials into the bull's-eye. If our children know and understand the essentials, they'll be prepared to offer grace to those who major on the minors and also be able to accept a wide variety of Christians with varying exterior beliefs.

The Bible Is a Community Book

Before the printing press was invented, people experienced the Bible in the context of community. Studying our Bible in solitude isn't wrong, but I fear we've lost a bit of its richness by merely studying it alone in what many call a "quiet time." We owe it to our children to study the Bible together, to let them ask questions, to engage with them over its pages.

We need to help our children understand how deeply community is woven into the fabric of the Bible. Many verses in the New Testament were meant for communities, but we have taken them out of context. Paul didn't write his letter to a Philippian, he wrote it to a gathering of Christ-followers in Philippi. He wrote Philippians 2:12-13 to a group of folks, not just one person. "Therefore, my dear friends, as you have always obeyed—not only in my presence, but now much more in my absence—continue to work out your salvation with fear and trembling, for it is God who works in you to will and to act according to his good purpose." Working out our salvation by ourselves is not enough because growth often happens in the context of community. What better community than the people God has placed under our roofs?

ॐ

The Bible is an amazing book, full of pathos and joy, tragedy and beauty, depression and hope. When we fall in love with its mysterious ambiguity, all the while following Jesus Christ, we impart to our children a holy awe for the Bible.

Part Three:

Releasing Children, Embracing Culture

Eventually, our children will leave our homes to live in this shifting culture. What does that mean? And how do we prepare them? We need to leave our children with three foundational truths: community, the kingdom of God, and gratitude.

Fourteen

A Community

Above all we need, particularly as children,
the reassuring presence of a visible community, an
intimate group that enfolds us with understanding
and love, and that becomes an object of our
spontaneous loyalty, as a criterion and point of
reference for the rest of the human race.

Lewis Mumford

Community is a buzzword of postmodernity. We long for authentic expressions of it. The world aches for it. Our children thrive in it. But finding community isn't always easy. A modern person might learn in an isolated ivory tower, but the postmodern best processes information and relationships through the context of community.

The problem with community is that it's usually sticky, painful, prickly. Patrick and I have often said that ministry would be a whole lot easier if only we didn't have to minister to people! And yet, through the difficulties of painful relationships, I've grown. Though I've been tempted to pull away from others because of past injuries, by God's grace I've been able to stay engaged. Teaching my children to do the same thing isn't easy. As a mom, I'd rather protect them from the inevitable barbs of others. But I can't. Jesus stayed within His community, daring to love even Judas. If I call myself a follower of Jesus, by His strength I can remain engaged, model humility and resilience, and pray my children catch those traits.

Community shapes our souls. The people around us sharpen our hearts, sand off our rough edges, and love us when we're unlovely. I venture to say we cannot grow in our walks with Jesus outside of it. If we isolate ourselves, our souls will atrophy.

However, community has gotten a bad reputation, and rightfully so. Nostalgic folks long for the "good old days" when neighborhoods fostered positive social pressure. Communities used to have unwritten rules requiring high standards from each child. If a parent was not around, community pressure would keep a kid in line. I call it the Old Mrs. Jones Factor. If Billy dashed into the middle of the street beyond the gaze of his mother, Old Mrs. Jones would stop him, scold him, and tell his mother. But that's no longer true.

I grew up in an unsafe community where my tricycle was stolen, my silver-dollar collection lifted, my innocence taken by older boys. Drugs passed hands. Break-ins were common. I was left to wander an unsafe neighborhood, always terrified. I learned the hard way that we can't necessarily trust our communities. So we have to create vibrant ones as havens in the midst of the darkness.

But how do we do that without completely isolating our children from the world Jesus longs to touch? This is not an easy predicament. We long to protect our children, and yet we know we need to prepare them for the world. The community that forms around our families is therefore of utter importance. Here are some ways to think about community in our families.

Welcome Rapscallions with a Caveat

Jesus formed a 12-person community around Himself. That community essentially became like a family. They traveled together, ate together, sang together, prayed together. Life filtered through these 12 men and Jesus. And yet one of them was a traitor. I am astounded that Jesus chose Judas and let him be a part. He knew Judas' heart, and yet He allowed him to be a part of the group's intimacy for three years. What a strange model for community! Why would Jesus allow that? Aside from the fact that Jesus knew the necessity of someone betraying Him in the grand scheme of the crucifixion, I wonder if Jesus wanted to teach His remaining 11 disciples something as a result.

Do you ever notice how much you learn from negative examples? We've been in ministry experiences where we were so flabbergasted by the behavior of other Christians that we took note, determining *not* to be like that. Perhaps that's what Jesus hoped for His disciples—that they'd see Judas' behavior and his death as a cautionary tale.

Does that mean we welcome rapscallions into our homes? Sometimes. Often we don't need to "welcome" them, they simply show up in our lives. People who steal. People who lie, cheat, and swindle. People who make promises and break them. People who are so needy they become codependent. Our children need to see us offer grace and tough love to scoundrels. If they never meet people like this, how will they develop an empathy for the lost?

Sometimes those difficult people are members of our extended families. You can't write them off—unless they pose a sincere danger to your children; then, by all means, cut off the relationship.[1] Many of them don't yet know Jesus, so we pray. We engage. We love. We welcome. We do this to show our kids that Jesus came to welcome all sorts of rascals like ourselves. Our children would not have the joy of praying for others and seeing God answer prayer if we shunned every difficult person who walked into our circle.

Know When to Intervene

Sometimes, however, God calls us to intervene in our children's lives because they have chosen a peer group that only negatively influences them. I'm not at all advocating we let our children find just any peer group. Wise parents train children to make wise choices. And when kids don't make good choices, particularly when they make friends who bring them down, parents need to step in. Postmodern culture is often full of folks who live on the slippery slopes of relativism, and this is not easy terrain to navigate.

Jesus allowed Judas into His circle of 12, but He didn't surround

Himself with Judases. And His closest circle of three friends didn't include the man who betrayed with kisses.

We do want our children to engage, but not so much that they lose their distinctiveness as followers of Jesus. Jesus said, "You are the salt of the earth. But if the salt loses its saltiness, how can it be made salty again? It is no longer good for anything, except to be thrown out and trampled by men" (Matthew 5:13). We need to teach our children the beauty and danger of this verse. Training them to engage and yet not lose saltiness is a difficult task. We need to help them see the fine line between loving those outside the circle of faith and longing to have lifestyles like those same folks.

It all boils down to irresistibility. Are we presenting Jesus as irresistible to our children? And have they experienced the dynamic, all-loving, radical Christ? If they have experienced Jesus in a life-changing way, they are apt to be change agents to their culture and are not likely to walk in relativism. We've been blessed to see our eldest daughter walk this line with grace. When she first met her friends in France, few of them knew Jesus. And yet Sophie influenced them. Mom after mom told me how her daughter looked up to Sophie and admired her. This is the kind of children we want to raise—those who engage rapscallions and everyday people and yet seem unsullied by their influence. Sophie does this because she is connected with Jesus through the community that surrounds her: our small church, our family, a peer group.

Let Them Spread Their Wings

Jesus not only welcomed Judas but also kept His disciples looking outward at the community around them. He didn't create a monastic following behind Palestinian walls. He sent His disciples out. He gathered an extended network of 72 followers and sent them in pairs ahead of Him. He warned them, "Go! I am sending you out like lambs among wolves" (Luke 10:3). I shudder to read those words. Every time I walk my children to school, I am keenly aware I am sending them out as little lambs amid howling predators. I have to believe that the prayers I lift to an all-powerful God follow them into that schoolyard.

I understand this is a controversial subject. As parents we are charged to protect our children, to give them space to be carefree and loved and playful. Some choose to homeschool. Some choose to send their children to private schools. Others send them to public institutions. I am not condemning any of those choices. The key to sending our children out is listening to God's voice. Patrick and I believed God wanted us to place our children in French public schools. We received a fair share of criticism about it. If we had felt God say something different, we would have done our best to obey. God sees all this. He knows our children better than we do. And He is bigger than our mistakes or wrong choices. Were we afraid when we sent them out? Terrified. Did God meet our children in the midst? Absolutely. Was it easy? Not at all. But we saw fruit.

What was the result of Jesus sending out disciples two by two? Fruit. "Lord, even the demons submit to us in your name" (Luke 10:17). The 72 had the privilege of seeing God show up. We've seen that in our family. By embracing the community around them, our children have seen friends come to Jesus. They've had to learn to pray more. They've wrestled through difficult relationships. They've watched God defend them. Though watching this process was excruciating at times, we've reveled in seeing our children return from their exploits, and we've been awed by God's faithfulness.

Embrace Kingdom Thinking

After sending out the 72, Jesus tells a story about a good Samaritan who dares to help a wounded Jew. The story was Jesus' answer to a question from an expert in Jewish law: "And who is my neighbor?" (Luke 10:29).

So Jesus tells the familiar story of how religious folk walk on by a wounded fellow Jew. He is eventually rescued by a Samaritan—someone the Jews hated. Here Jesus expands our community outward. Our neighbor is someone in need. He equates our desire to help others with the kingdom of God. The more we think of God's kingdom and the reward He gives in heaven, the more apt we are to show kindness to strangers, to help the oppressed, to love those who are unlovely. Jesus said, "For I was hungry and you gave me something to eat, I was thirsty and you gave me something to drink, I was a stranger and you invited me in, I needed clothes and you clothed me, I was sick and you looked after me, I was in prison and you came to visit me" (Matthew 25:35-36).

If we can instill a kingdom mind-set in our children, they will naturally expand their view of community. Their neighbors will be people who need to see the love of Jesus. In that way, our smaller communities of faith expand because we are continually reaching out to those who don't yet know Jesus.

Theme-Park Christianity

Our friend Justus, a youth pastor who joined our church-planting team in France, sees a shift in youth ministry. For a long time, youth ministry was what he calls "theme-park Christianity." It used to be okay to throw a ball and play a record (gasp! How old do I seem with that reference!) in a youth setting. But youth became more complicated, more techno-savvy. Suddenly that wasn't enough. Youth ministry became entertainment. Laser tag. Trips to Disneyland. State-of-the-art sound systems that blared edgy yet appropriate music. This is what reached students.

But all that is shifting. Postmodern kids want experience. They want their lives to count for something. They're weary of nonstop entertainment. So what do they do? The new wave of youth ministry is to take kids on mission trips—to expand their idea of the world community. Justus also had his students participate in the 30-hour famine sponsored by World Vision.[2] Together, they fasted. They had to go to the store on a very tight (virtual) budget and try to buy enough food to feed a family for a month. They prayed for those who were without. They applied for welfare benefits. This experience helped kids see that life is more than mere entertainment.

We can open our children to the realities of poverty as well. We can take them with us on short mission trips. In France we hosted a mission team from Texas. One of the team's eight members, Kevin, was ten years old. He told us, "I came on this trip because I wanted to understand missions better." Kevin's parents are preparing him to see the world through wider lenses.

Revel in the Beauty of People

People amaze my friend Ann. She's well-suited for her human resources job. She told me she could listen to people for hours because she finds them so fascinating. I pray my children will hold the same amazement. To revel in the beauty of another human. To find people from all different backgrounds and economic statuses interesting.

Heather, a missionary in Madrid, recently had a homeless woman stay in her house. "It was interesting watching my kids interact with her. My kids thought she was our babysitter. This is how they view guests. My kids trust us, and they believe everyone in our home is trustworthy, but the homeless person wasn't trustworthy. I had to tell them to be guarded around her." Heather's children have a fascination about people, so much so that they treated the homeless person as a prized guest and wanted her to babysit. Why do they have this fascination? Because Heather and her husband Troy welcome a wide variety of people in their home and treat them as friends, not outsiders. They treat the people they meet with dignity, and their children are following their example.

We had a barbecue the day after our first church service in France. People from all walks of life came: teachers, musicians, managers, government employees, entrepreneurs, stay-at-home moms, jet-setters, students. We gathered around a genuine Texas barbecue, getting to know each other while country music filled the background. My children met new folks. Sophie told me, "Mom, I'm so pleased that so many different people have come today." She's learning to appreciate the beauty of different people.

What If There Were No Youth Groups or Children's Ministries?

We faced this in France. Our church was in its infancy, so we had to wrestle with helping our children become spiritually formed without the benefit of programs. This got me wondering. What would parents do without youth groups or children's ministries? Have those communities become crutches, relieving parents of the responsibility of embracing the first community God has placed us in—the family? Psalm 68:6 says, "God sets the lonely in families." He has strategically placed us in families as our first realm of community. I fear we've forsaken the importance of this.

Many value family time for this very reason—to be the initial influence in a child's soul care, to establish family as the bedrock for a child's life. Family is perhaps the most realistic community. We rage. We cry. We hope. We injure. We forgive. We grow. We change. We give. We take. And through all of this, we learn how to love people who differ from us. To the extent that we teach children to exist in harmony in their family of origin, we teach them to adequately navigate any community they enter.

What if we didn't have any church programs? Consider that for a moment. What if you were solely responsible to create a haven of community in your home? Who would you bring into the circle? How would you train your children? The nurture of our children's souls is our responsibility. We are their first community, so how can we create a community of grace that helps them understand the heart of God in the midst of a crazy world? And how can we become an irresistible infrastructure that children outside our family—our children's friends—gravitate toward?

Find a Good Church

Stick around life long enough and you'll find paradox. Yes, our families need to be irresistible communities where our children learn about Jesus. Yes, we are responsible to train our children. But we need others. We can't do this parenting thing alone, nor should we try. Intact communities once thrived outside our front doors. Multigenerational families often lived within easy driving distance from one another. If a crisis came, the extended family would huddle around, offering support when most needed. Some today have this. I'm reminded of my

Aunt Fran's family. Her extended family is available for each other through triumph and tears.

We need church. We need the body of Christ to help us raise our children. We need support when we feel as if we're sinking. We need meals when we're sick. One of the most important things we can do for our children is find a good church—one where each family member is a stakeholder, where everyone feels connected somehow. Remember, though, that no church is perfect. Some families float here and there, looking for a perfect church, and never commit. Every church has weaknesses and flaws, as do families. Yet God blesses us as we choose to be a part of a body of imperfect believers.

We were blessed to go to Lake Pointe Church while Patrick attended seminary. These people became our family. I remember telling the Lord once, "I will never go to a megachurch," and since I grew up in the Northwest, where nondenominational churches reigned supreme, I added, "And please don't send me to a Southern Baptist church." Be careful what you tell the Almighty! Lake Pointe is a megachurch with 10,000 or so of our friends, and it is Southern Baptist. I love God's sense of humor!

Our children made many friends there. Sunday school teachers helped build character into their lives. The people in the Adult Bible Fellowship we pastored became our closest friends. With them, we served others—our children alongside us. We spent a day cleaning debris from a yard of a fellow church member who was dying of brain cancer. One of our members, Mike, was dying himself, but he chose to help, digging bulbs through labored breaths. Our children had the privilege of knowing and loving these people. When our friend with brain cancer died, they mourned. When Mike passed from earth to heaven, they took part in helping his widow. Nothing can replace that kind of community.

I firmly believe God led us to that church. A team of dear people from Lake Pointe flew at their own expense to France to serve. They were tireless. They were generous. They loved our children. They proved to be examples of servanthood. Our children watched and absorbed that—all because we had the privilege of attending that church.

Almost monthly we received care packages from people at church. Folks sent us e-mails and letters telling us they were praying for us. As we lived on the outpost in France, with a church in its infancy, we experienced more of the body of Christ than we thought possible. I felt spoiled and overloved. And so did our children. God taught me about true community even when it was miles and miles away.

The apostle Paul said, "But in fact God has arranged the parts in the body, every one of them, just as he wanted them to be" (1 Corinthians 12:18). God is in the business of arranging us into local bodies of believers. He blesses us through our faith relationships. He provides community for us through our local church. Our children benefit from that community, sometimes more than we do. If you aren't a part of a local body of believers, trust that God will lead you to the faith community you need—and that needs you. Be careful though. Sometimes He sends you to the most unexpected communities—like Southern Baptist megachurches...or France!

❧

As I look back on the times of extreme growth in my relationship with Jesus, I see community. Oftentimes, the messiness of community, and my participation in it, drove me to my knees. I've had to learn how to remove the log in my eye to see the splinter in others'. I've had to humble myself and ask for forgiveness. I've had to say difficult things to friends who no longer remained friends after the conversation. I've watched as people self-imploded. I've ached with others who have run from Jesus. But I have grown.

If I'm honest, I would rather protect my children from the negative side of community. I'd rather hide them somewhere so they wouldn't have to experience the barbs. But I'd be doing them a disservice. I'd shelter them far too much, crippling them for life.

The story's been told of a young person happening upon a cocoon.

Tenderly, she pulled away the strings of the cocoon strand by strand, helping the butterfly emerge. She rejoiced as the butterfly unfurled its wings, only to be disappointed that a few hours later it died. The butterfly needed the struggle to survive. It needed to push against the pain, to wrestle with the knots surrounding its eager wings. Without the struggle, the wings wouldn't be strong enough to fly.

I wonder how many of us pull away the cocoon, crippling our children's ability to fly. I wonder how much we sacrifice on the altar of protectionism. Community is hard. But we must be willing to let our children struggle through it so they can build wings with stamina and learn to fly.

Fifteen

A Kingdom

People will come from east and west
and north and south, and will take their
places at the feast in the kingdom of God.

LUKE 13:29

The concept of the kingdom of God can be hard to grasp because the metaphor of kingdom isn't something we readily relate to. Though my youngest daughter is sure she should be a princess someday and my son is deeply rooted in the knight tradition in his play, none of us really understand it because we don't live in kingdoms anymore. Many of our societies are based on individual rights, allowing each citizen to have a say. Presidents, heads of state, and executives tend to be representatives of a whole society. Even where kings reign, they are often merely figureheads, surrounded by a majority of opinions.

In our world, everyone has a say. Many have rights. No one person has absolute power. How that translates to the gospel is uncanny. We stress the fact that Jesus set us free from our sins. We use the metaphor of being released from the slavery of Egypt, entering into the promised land of skinniness in our dieting programs. We're all about kingdoms that directly benefit us. But what about verses like these?

> • "Obey them not only to win their favor when their eye is on you, but like slaves of Christ, doing the will of God from your heart" (Ephesians 6:6).

- "Anyone who does not take his cross and follow me is not worthy of me. Whoever finds his life will lose it, and whoever loses his life for my sake will find it" (Matthew 10:38–39).

- "Whoever wants to become great among you must be your servant, and whoever wants to be first must be slave of all. For even the Son of Man did not come to be served, but to serve, and to give his life as a ransom for many" (Mark 10:43-45).

Jesus calls us—whether we like the way His kingdom works or not—to die, to become slaves. His kingdom is about His rule over our lives and our willingness to truly say, pray, and mean "Thy kingdom come." We let those words roll off our tongues, but do we really know what they mean in everyday life? How can we parent our children in a postmodern world as we happily follow the kingdom of God? And how can that way of sacrificial living be attractive to our children?

If I were to summarize the way most of us parent our children, I would have to say this: We primarily parent—and dare I say *live our lives*—to reduce pain and increase prosperity. We protect our children from the radical call of Christ because, to be honest, truly following after His kingdom messes with our plans. It's difficult. Painful. It could mean giving up wealth. After Jesus gave His mandate to the rich young ruler, "the disciples were amazed at his words. But Jesus said again, 'Children, how hard it is to enter the kingdom of God!'" (Mark 10:24). We live as if entering the kingdom were no more difficult than standing in line at the grocery store, when in reality it is life-altering and sometimes bewildering. It costs.

The Kingdom of God—in France?

I confess I haven't always followed after my King in radical obedience. I prefer routine. I like comfort. I enjoy not worrying about money. I love avoiding pain. I'd rather be a slave to the mundane than a slave of Christ. But as Bonhoeffer says, "When Christ calls a man, he bids him come and die."[1]

I faced that very mandate as we made our decision to move our family to France. Though I feigned obedience on the outside, my insides recoiled at the thought of moving halfway around the world to a nation whose language was only vaguely familiar. I worried about my children nearly every minute.

Am I ruining their lives? Will they end up resenting Jesus because of our choices? Will they be crushed in the French schooling system? Will I be able to parent well in another country? Will moving rip apart my family? Will I ruin my career?

I loved my life in Dallas. We had a happy home, great schools, good friends, people who spoke into our lives. We had ministries we loved, neighbors we adored, a safe place to live. We attended an amazing church. Our children played on church sport teams, went to Sunday school, and attended camps. We had two cars, a big house, nice things. We lived the American dream. To begin to think of living the American dream in reverse—to actively choose a different lifestyle when we "had it all"—messed with my heart.

I'm certainly not suggesting that to follow Christ means everyone has to move to another country, but in our case, that was Christ's call to "die." I rebelled. I wept. When we were ready to move, I freaked out. I was so trying to be the obedient Christian wife that I hadn't shared my heart with Patrick until right before our moving container arrived. The truth, when I let it all out, was that I flat out did not want to go, didn't want to put my children through it, didn't want to go through it myself. I wanted to stay home.

I worked through that, and we landed in France. Little did I know that merely moving away was the least of our worries, as the first year of our missionary experience careened out of control. Our children didn't learn the language in three months as others had assured they would. They wept going to school. They wept at school. They wept after school. Our church-planting team faltered. Sadness after struggle after heartache assaulted our family.

Bewildered, I wanted to move home.

I didn't want to follow the call of Christ if this is what it meant. I missed my friends. I missed being able to communicate in my heart language. Sometimes I still ask God if I could please follow my own prescribed kingdom, where everyone was happy, no one suffered, and no injustice was done to us. Above all the worries was my stress about my dear children, who were suffering because of our decision. I found no reassurance that everything would turn out fine in the end, despite the promise of Romans 8:28. I knew too much about the danger of pulling that promise from its context, dismembering it from the difficult words of verse 29: "For those God foreknew he also predestined to be conformed to the likeness of his Son, that he might be the firstborn among many brothers." I knew Christ's process of making us conformed to Himself was not merely a pretty phrase. Being conformed to Christ's image is an excruciating process because Jesus was obedient to the point of death.

Death. I hate that word. It means the end of security, familiarity. It's the end of everything easy and known.

The height of my discouragement, particularly about my children, came when I read a missionary newsletter from a church-planting family who had been in France for decades. Almost as a postscript, they added at the very end a sentence like this: "Please pray for our children. None of them are walking closely with Jesus." The words stabbed me, ripping through the tender, breaking flesh of my mother heart. Did I bring my kids to France to squelch their desire for Jesus? To kill their relationship with Him?

God in His tenderness sent Nancy and Cyndi to our home to watch our children while we went to our mission's leadership summit. When Cyndi arrived home in Dallas, she sent me this e-mail, not knowing my turmoil:

> All three of your kids are so remarkable. They are learning to push through, lean on Jesus, and come out on the other side stronger and smiling. I saw it all week last week. I was amazed. Your whole life there, to me, is such a testament

to God's order, beauty, sufficiency, strength, grace, energy, and excellence. I have been tempted to settle for mediocrity in certain areas of my life and came back from France challenged. Thank you! God is poised to move in a mighty way, I can feel it. He has been moving, positioning, rumbling all along, but I feel it is only a hint of what's to come.

Her words were water to a parched heart. Sometimes God asks us to wait until heaven to receive the treasures of obedience. And sometimes in His mercy, He encourages us on earth with e-mails from Cyndi. Our obedience cost our children a lot. It cost us a lot. And yet God has been big enough to shoulder their stress and pain as they live in His kingdom.

What Is the Gospel, Really?

We need to ask ourselves, what exactly is the gospel? Jesus said He came for several purposes—including to share the good news of the kingdom of God with the lost and to destroy the devil. "I must preach the good news of the kingdom of God to the other towns also, because that is why I was sent" (Luke 4:43). "The reason the Son of God appeared was to destroy the devil's work" (1 John 3:8). In postmodern circles, a tension exists between seeing these two purposes fulfilled.

In evangelical circles, sharing the gospel has more to do with telling people about Jesus, about helping people come to grips with the claims of Christ and understanding their inherent need for a Savior. In more liberal circles of the church, sharing the gospel is measured by how we as believers are abolishing the evils of society—racism, poverty, war, starvation. What if we could marry these perspectives? I realize that's a simplistic answer, but consider the implications.

What if we lived out the gospel so that people could *see* aspects of the kingdom of God as we proclaimed it? What if we proclaimed Jesus *and* lived out His principles?

The Social Gospel—a Bad Rap?

One part of the armor of God is a pair of peace shoes: "...and with your feet fitted with the readiness that comes from the gospel of peace" (Ephesians 6:15). I've sometimes forgotten that Jesus is the Prince of Peace. He grieves at man's inhumanity to man. He weeps as He sees genocide, war, disease. He loves those who are needy and weak, assigning them a special place in the kingdom. "Blessed are the poor in spirit, for theirs is the kingdom of heaven" (Matthew 5:3). Jesus said that when we love those who suffer, we love Him.[2]

How do we model a lived-out gospel? One that welcomes the downtrodden and needy? This postmodern world is wildly attracted to people who dare to love the unlovely. They applaud the Mother Teresas of the world. They support Bono's causes. They see Darfur's genocide and weep.

For too long we've viewed the world as "out there." "They" are those not in our circle of believing friends—those people we "target" to bring into our fold. We have received missionary support letters that speak of *those* people in not-so-glowing terms. What if there is another way? What if we bring these folks along with us as we do the kingdom work of ministering to AIDS patients? Joseph Myers, in his astute book *The Search to Belong*, knocks this notion that folks have to believe something in order to belong. What if we allowed *those* people to belong before they believed? What if we beckoned them to Jesus as we lived the Christian life alongside them?

Lisa and Will Samson have a heart for social justice issues, and they've included their children in the adventure. They attended an outdoor sleepover in their community sponsored by those who were upset about the Northern Ugandan children forced to take up arms. Lisa shared their experience:

> We left the house a little after seven, sleeping bags, pillows and backpacks in tow. Banners and signs surrounded the park, their wooden sticks poked into the turf and we chose a spot under some trees. It was drizzling on and off. The organizers were really glad to see an actual family show up! The rain held off to just the occasional spritz and I prayed it would continue to

hold back. We'd decided we'd stick it out no matter what when we considered what the kids in Uganda go through each night! The drip of rain on my sleeping bag awakened me around 5:35. Will ran back to our house to get the car around 5:50 while I gathered the kids and our drippy things. We loaded up and were home by 6:10.

I felt a part of something important, and even better, the kids did too. I am grateful God gave us the opportunity to help us help them learn how to care for His people, particularly His children in northern Uganda. My daughter, Gwynnie, said a couple of times, "I'm glad this isn't happening here. I'm glad kids over here don't have to fight."

I told her, "But those children are every bit as precious as the kids over here, Gwynnie." And we cried a little bit. Watching these college students pray, be together, write letters, and care enabled me to see the face of a loving God over and over again. Perhaps, if Ty and Jake and Gwynnie live a life of justice, they will grow up seeing God's face over and over again too. Maybe the answers to their questions about God's role in caring for His children won't be so hard won because they've consistently seen Him in action.[3]

JR and Ginger Vassar have encouraged their daughter Neeley as she's seen poverty on the streets of New York.

Our children are very aware of the needy people in the city. We see homeless people frequently wherever we go. Neeley sees these needs and responds with a heart of compassion. We allow her to give out McDonald's gift cards to those she feels impressed to help. Neeley has also chosen to use her own money to buy them. Recently, she went with JR and a group from our church to give out blankets and gift cards to homeless people. She came home with such a concern for the people she met. She prayed that night for a mute man to get his voice back and for a homeless family. She even prayed for a homeless dog.

Allowing children to give freely from their hearts—as the Vassars did here—helps to break the hold of materialism on them—a key component to the social aspect of the gospel. There is more to life than things and money. Jesus told us to have purses with holes so that the resources He blesses us with can spill over into the lives of the less fortunate.

What the Gospel Is For

My friend Justin is a church planter in Paris. For several weeks, he received e-mails from well-meaning friends full of concern for his spiritual well-being. From their perspective, Justin and his wife Jen were not adequately living out the kingdom of God because they were not proclaiming Jesus in a specified way. Very discouraged, Justin wrestled with the e-mails. He wondered if his friends were right. He worried that he hadn't said enough appropriate words about Jesus.

But then something happened. One of Justin's non-believing friends broke up with his girlfriend. In desperation, he called on Justin—someone he felt safe with. Justin was Jesus to this friend.

Another friend met with him over many hours in a smoke-filled bar. In this setting, Justin shared Jesus with his friend, but not in the typical evangelical way. He welcomed questions. He let his friend wrestle. He spoke about the kingdom of God: "I talked about how the kingdom of God is a story and God has invited us to play a role. Maybe," Justin said, "our part is service—making a difference in the world around us."[4] He presented the gospel in terms of what it was instead of what it wasn't.

So many times, we define for others and for our children what the great and amazing life-giving gospel is not:

- Following Jesus means you're against abortion.
- Being a Christ-follower means you're against homosexuality.
- Loving Jesus means you can't possibly align yourself with liberal American politics.

We've become so accustomed to what we are not—as has our society—that we've lost what we are for. So Justin shared what a world infused with Jesus would look like. He shared what the gospel was *for*—peace between people, utterly changed hearts, people who care about injustice, a world without hunger. He didn't demand his friend say a specific prayer. He simply listened and shared.

Amid the cacophony of the accusatory e-mails, Justin smiled after one of his rendezvous. "I've never had my Bible smell like cigarettes before," he said after his encounter with his friend. I wonder how many of us could say the same thing? That we dared to live in the margins of society to share an amazing, wild God with broken people? I wonder how well we are preparing our children to actually live the positive message of the gospel in the midst of a difficult, smoky culture? Are we helping our children love those who frequent bars? Or are we cordoning them off, subjugating them to Christian enclaves with Christian music, Christian friends, Christian candy, Christian clothing, Christian dolls, Christian DVDs, Christian tea? How will they ever be irresistible representations of Jesus if we don't train them?

Jesus said not to hide our lights under a bushel, but I fear we as parents are not only doing that in our own lives, happy with our own subculture of nicety, but we are isolating our children as well. We have domesticated God, making Him as easy to swallow as chewable Tylenol. And the grand beauty of the kingdom of God has been lost.

Parents are afraid, and rightly so. Outside our doors is a plethora of social ills—murder, sexual abuse, drugs, promiscuity. We are right to protect the innocence of childhood. But I fear that we have forgotten the greater mandate. In our fear, we have lived our lives in safety. And we've taken our children alongside. How will a frenetic protectionism help our children interact with a fallen world? Will separating ourselves from the surrounding culture help our children be better Christ followers?

My friends Jeanne and George Damoff have engaged the surrounding culture in their home:

Because George taught college-aged students who often visited our home, our children grew up in an atmosphere of intelligent discussion and friendly debate. Over the years we "adopted" two missionary kids who'd grown up in Italy, had half a dozen college students live with us (one at a time), and ministered in our home to individuals who'd been involved in Satanism, suffered child sexual abuse, or battled severe depression. We didn't always let our kids know the particulars of these people's lives, but we did allow them to participate in our family's outreach to them.[5]

Tim Kimmel calls our withdrawal from the surrounding culture our "Christian parallel universe." The further away we remove our families from the surrounding culture, the less we are like lights to the world. And he believes that engagement produces a deeper intimacy with Christ in our children: "When families are committed to being this light, they are inclined to live more intimately with Christ. They pray more, they study their Bibles more, they care for one another more, they reach out to their neighbors more."[6] We saw this phenomenon lived out in our family in a secular nation more than we ever did in the Bible belt.

Sophie—Living for the Kingdom

I saw our eldest daughter, Sophie, change in tremendous ways when she moved from our protected world in Dallas, where all her friends knew Jesus, to a secular society, where none of her friends followed Christ and most were atheists. When I asked her if she'd like to go back to the states and live, she said, "Yes, in some ways. But I wouldn't want to live there forever. People there are so narrow-minded. Everyone in my circle was a Christian. I actually like having non-Christian friends."

You'd think Patrick and I would panic that our 13-year-old daughter had no Christian friends. But by God's grace, Sophie became a catalyst in her surroundings. She lived Jesus in front of her friends and even her enemies. She learned how to lean on God. Instead of her friends enticing her into a sinful, selfish lifestyle, she worked to lift them up. When she helped lead one of her friends to Jesus, she said, "Mom, I've never felt God's presence so closely as when I saw my friend ask questions and get close to Jesus."

No amount of isolation would have prepared her for that moment. She learned to live the kingdom of God in the midst of her mission field. This was humbling to watch. Our first convert in France was Sophie's friend. And her friend's parents soon began asking questions about Jesus.

Aidan—Jesus, Cupcake Money, and Judo

The Sermon on the Mount is alive and well in Aidan's life. I watched as he lived it out before me. One day I picked up Julia and Aidan at school while the clouds poured cold, wet tears. It was the day the school raised money for charity, so we had sent good ol' American cupcakes to sell for one euro each. The proceeds went to help poor children.

I had given each child two euros. Julia cried when I saw her. "Mommy," she said, "my teacher didn't let me buy cake." So, drenched as we were, we walked over to the cake-selling area. She bought two cupcakes—ours and my friend Kate's. Julia couldn't balance them well, so Aidan offered his plate. (If a man needs a coat, offer him yours.)[7] Then he sheltered the plate under his blue umbrella all the way home.

I noticed he had one piece of cake. "Yeah," he said. "I decided that I'd buy two and then see if someone needed one. I noticed that my friend Remy didn't have a piece, so I gave him one of mine. He liked it." (Blessed are the merciful.)

Seeing Jesus in your children is a beautiful thing, like a snapshot-glimpse of heaven. While torrents of water puddled in our yard, I was warmed knowing Aidan gave what he had to bless someone else, with no thought of reward.

It's not always roses, though. Aidan had his share of deep struggle in France. He was ridiculed in class. He was shunned by classmates. He cried at night because he had a hard time making friends. And he struggled with judo. The teacher allowed the kids to attack and tackle each other. Aidan is also uncomfortable with the chants the teacher does before the judo lesson. He hates getting pummelled by other kids, and perhaps even more, he hates tackling others. One day he told Patrick that he didn't want to go to judo. He begged his father to please let him opt out for the rest of the year. Patrick replied, "I can pull you out, or you can stay in there and endure and see if God wants to teach you any lesson in the midst of it." Aidan stayed. It still wasn't easy. He learned how to endure difficulties, something that will help him navigate the postmodern world outside his home.

Julia—the Joyful Phone Call

Being engaged in the culture and embracing mission eventually led to Julia meeting Jesus. We'd been praying for someone in our circle of friends who was struggling with anxiety disorders and possible demonic oppression. Ever since we started praying, Julia had a difficult time. She'd disobey often, whine incessantly, and act out inappropriately. Whenever a particular song about Jesus freeing a demoniac played, she asked me to turn it off—immediately. I asked her what was bothering her.

"I'm hearing mean voices," she told me.

"What kind of voices?" I tried not to let panic rise to my throat.

"They tell me to do mean things," she cried. "Like kick my brother or whine. Sometimes they wake me up in the night. They're scary."

I told her about Jesus and saying His name out loud when the voices bothered her, but she still struggled. Later I realized that all of her symptoms coincided with our prayers for our friend.

In the midst of Julia hearing voices, we had to leave for our leadership summit in Portugal. As I mentioned earlier, Nancy and Cyndi— along with Cyndi's daughter Bethany—gave us the gift of watching our children. We briefed them about Julia.

While we were gone, Julia had a difficult day. She screamed. She cried. She got angry. Bethany, Cyndi's 12-year-old daughter, was babysitting her during this rampage. She asked if Julia wanted to talk. Julia nodded.

Julia shared about the voices again.

"You know you can pray and ask Jesus to help you," Bethany said.

Julia cried. "I have done that a million billion times, and they are still there!"

"Have you ever given your life to Jesus?" Bethany asked.

"No, but I'd like to," Julia said.

Bethany led Julia in a prayer. She made her a certificate—something Julia clutched all that day. One of the most beautiful voice mails I'd ever received was this one we listened to in Lisbon: "Mommy, Daddy, I wanted to let you know that today, I invited Jesus into my life." Patrick and I cried when we heard her tender voice.

When we returned, I asked her if she heard any voices in her head anymore. "Yes," she said.

I shuddered. "What do they say?"

"Well, it's different," she said. "It tells me to make wise choices and to be kind."

I smiled. The God of the universe has taken up residence in Julia's life, speaking words of encouragement and kindness to her. And He chose to do that against the backdrop of a difficult ministry situation in a very dark country.

Spiritual Warfare and the Kingdom

Mention the word *kingdom*, and inevitably warfare comes to mind. We saw firsthand spiritual warfare played out in Julia's struggle. So often I forget that a very real battle is being waged in the heavens. A battle for souls. A battle for the minds of our children. The enemy of our lives, Satan, wants to steal from us, dampen our fervency for Jesus, and destroy our families. We forget the furor of this verse: "For our struggle is not against flesh and blood, but against the rulers, against the authorities, against the powers of this dark world and against the spiritual forces of evil in the heavenly realms" (Ephesians 6:12).

It's a battle, requiring much prayer, much attention, much joy in the midst of it. We pray for our children as they go out into their worlds. We pray with them for their friends who don't yet know Jesus. We pray for those caught in Satan's traps, for their release. And through it all, we recognize the beauty of God sitting sovereign on His throne, knowing He is greater than any demonic force.

As we engaged in the culture God placed us in, we saw the intensity of the battle increase. I didn't realize how thick the battle was until I flew home to Dallas. When I landed and went through customs, I felt a lightness of soul I hadn't experienced in months. When I returned to France, the moment we touched down in Nice, the heaviness returned. I wept for a few days. I asked prayer-loving folks to pray for me. I understood afresh that the kingdom of God, as it advances, attracts the enemy's attention.

Modeling the Kingdom

Perhaps more important than merely engaging the people outside our door is modeling a kingdom mind-set in our homes. Our children followed us overseas. They watched us give sacrificially. They observed our interactions with others. They prayed with us. They prayed for us. They caught the kingdom because they saw how very real it is to us, though we often fall down. Jeanne and George Damoff have also modeled this mind-set.

> We could have talked about the importance of this forever, but if they didn't see us praying, giving generously, taking people into our home, reaching out to the needy in our own community, our words would have been empty. As it is, our college-aged son plans to go to seminary when he graduates from Wheaton next year, with an ultimate goal of possibly moving to Japan. Our daughter majored in theology, is fluent in Spanish, and is interested in South American missions. They've both been involved in ministries to the poor, separate from our family's outreaches.[8]

Imparting a kingdom mind-set is best done through example. It's caught, not taught. Our children will trust the sincerity of our words if they observe our integrity. Just remember, the mission field is right outside your front door, wherever you live.

We Are the Kingdom

Jesus used many metaphors to describe the kingdom of God. He likened it to seed scattered on the ground, a prodigal returning home, a coin found by a joyful widow. Consider this illustration: "What shall we say the kingdom of God is like, or what parable shall we use to describe it? It is like a mustard seed, which is the smallest seed you plant in the ground. Yet when planted, it grows and becomes the largest of all the garden plants, with such big branches that the birds of the air can perch in its shade" (Mark 4:30-32).

How small are we when we're conceived? How small were our children? Specks. Microscopic. And yet look at our children today! They have grown from infancy to toddlerhood to childhood. Their skeletons have stretched exponentially from the time God formed them in the womb. Their minds have grasped deeper and deeper truths. What if Jesus was speaking here about us? That we are the mustard seeds? Our lives for the kingdom start small, but as the Holy Spirit invigorates us, as He waters and fertilizes our souls, we begin to grow. Our families started as tiny seeds. Could it be that God is using the microcosm of our families to radically expand the kingdom of God? Could it be that as we raise our children in a godly, authentic home, we are actively expanding the kingdom?

God has planted our children in our homes for a reason. He has entrusted them to us. We have the privilege of partnering with a mighty God to tend these seedlings. By God's grace, we see the beauty of their growth. And we long to see birds nest in their branches as the kingdom expands.

Sixteen

A Gift

Do you see what we've got? An unshakable king-
dom! And do you see how thankful we
must be? Not only thankful, but brimming
with worship, deeply reverent before God.
For God is not an indifferent bystander.

HEBREWS 12:28 MSG

A big tear slopped down Aidan's face. He hung his head. "I'm sorry," he muttered.

Patrick and I were reprimanding him for not being grateful. The day started off well. We were on the cusp of our first church service in France. Aidan wanted to help set up, but we were so busy, we couldn't find a suitable job for him. So he found the coffee makers and unpacked them. Soon, though, he became bored and asked for more jobs. We brushed him aside. This contributed to his angry attitude. When he got to the children's ministry, he was in a foul mood. Instead of participating, he stood aloof to the side. He rolled his eyes. "Bo-ring," he said, loud enough for the teacher to hear it.

When we talked to him about it, he regretted his actions. We told him how we wanted him to learn to be grateful and express that thankfulness to the people who were teaching him. He agreed. We know he's a sweet boy who often expresses gratitude. But he's so much like us.

We forget sometimes.

We roll our eyes.

We say "bo-ring" under our breath.

We treat life as if it were all about us.

But the essence of life is gratitude. Thankfulness.

How do we instill gratefulness in our children while the world around them is spinning on the axis of selfishness? One of the greatest compliments we've received as parents came from friends who visited us. They'd had a week to observe us in all our normal glory: bickering, frustration, smiles, tears, raised voices, hushed voices. At the end of their time, one said, "The thing that strikes me about your children is how grateful they are, how thankful they are for everything." Hearing this salved my heart. Somehow, someway, we've helped our children understand that life is a gift, and God its giver.

So much of what we try to teach our children is demonstrated, not preached. Perhaps our children are grateful because we are grateful. Or maybe they've seen others be selfish, and it rubs them the wrong way. Or maybe they've gotten to know the gentleness of Jesus a little more each day.

Teaching kids that life is a gift isn't easy. There are no surefire formulas. But I can give you a glimpse into our feeble attempts to instill and demonstrate gratefulness.

Elevate Their Eyes

God is the one who elevates us. He lifts our heads above circumstances. In Psalm 3:3, the psalmist says, "But you are a shield around me, O LORD; you bestow glory on me and lift up my head." Why does He lift our heads? So we can see the vista beyond our belly buttons. Above us is heaven, where the Triune God reigns in glory. An interesting passage in Philippians shows the dichotomy between living for this earth and seeking a heavenly perspective.

> Join with others in following my example, brothers, and take note of those who live according to the pattern we gave you. For, as I have often told you before and now say again even with tears, many live as enemies of the cross

of Christ. Their destiny is destruction, their god is their stomach, and their glory is in their shame. Their mind is on earthly things (Philippians 3:17-19).

Paul shows the importance of being worthy of being followed. He set the example of grateful living and operating with an eternal perspective. He warns of those who live only for themselves, whose minds are securely anchored to this earth.

Paul continues his thought with the word *but,* connoting a contrast. "But our citizenship is in heaven. And we eagerly await a Savior from there, the Lord Jesus Christ, who, by the power that enables him to bring everything under his control, will transform our lowly bodies so that they will be like his glorious body" (Philippians 3:20-21). If we as parents can live that way, eagerly, as if on tiptoes, straining to hear the music of heaven in the mundane of life, perhaps our children will catch that vision. The truth is that Jesus is coming again. And one day we will be part of the new heavens and the new earth. Someday, God will reward us for everything we did for the sake of Jesus—every unseen act, every time we endured persecution with joy or chose not to gossip. We clearly see meaning in this life when we look through the lens of eternal perspective.

When we were on the cusp of moving to France, I read *Safely Home* by Randy Alcorn to my two oldest children. It's the story of the persecuted church in China, told from an earthly and heavenly perspective. I wanted my children to understand persecution because I knew they'd experience it in France. I wanted them to know that this life is a gift, and we must use it to its fullest. The more we live it for Jesus, the more we rejoice in heaven, and the more crowns we may cast at His scarred, beautiful feet.

Gratitude and eternal perspective share a great connection. I marvel at how seamlessly Paul weaves these together:

> Be very careful, then, how you live—not as unwise but as wise, making the most of every opportunity, because the days are evil. Therefore do not be foolish, but understand what the Lord's will is. Do not get drunk on wine,

which leads to debauchery. Instead, be filled with the Spirit. Speak to one another with psalms, hymns and spiritual songs. Sing and make music in your heart to the Lord, always giving thanks to God the Father for everything, in the name of our Lord Jesus Christ (Ephesians 5:15-20).

Paul reminds us that life is short, that there's more to life than simply ticking things off a to-do list. He tells us to be careful, to live life through the power of the Spirit of God for the sake of the next life. And then he talks about thankfulness.

Walking the kids home from school after our first worship service the weekend before, I was amazed at how well God provided. So I sang a simple chorus of Alleluias and He is holys. The kids joined in. We skipped. We saw God move. We glimpsed a hint of heaven, and then we celebrated.

Instilling an eternal perspective, a longing for heaven, in our children is not as easy as taking a blue pill in *The Matrix*. In the movie, simply swallowing the right pill tore away the veil between the real world and the Real World. In our everyday lives, pulling away the veil is not so simple. We must demonstrate it on the field of our own insecurity and weakness.

But we have this treasure in jars of clay to show that this all-surpassing power is from God and not from us. We are hard pressed on every side, but not crushed; perplexed, but not in despair; persecuted, but not abandoned; struck down, but not destroyed. We always carry around in our body the death of Jesus, so that the life of Jesus may also be revealed in our body (2 Corinthians 4:7-10).

As we endure life's hardships with grace, knowing that our little deaths on this earth bring big rewards in heaven, we tear away a bit of that mysterious veil, hopefully slaking the thirst of our children who have that same longing. Randy Alcorn has said we were created for a person and a place—the person is Jesus, the place, heaven. How much do you long for Jesus? And how often do you think of this life in terms of heaven and its reward? The more we demonstrate both, the more we will skip through this life with gratefulness.

Worship God

We sing worship songs together as a family. The sweetest voices I've heard have been the choruses of my children, eyes closed, chins lifted toward heaven, belting songs of beauty to the one who made all beauty. This year one of my goals has been to do chores to worship music. I haven't done a very good job at it yet, but I'm trying. I'm exploring the link between singing or listening to elevating songs and doing work and life cheerfully. The clouds of despair dissipate.

God placed us on this earth to worship and revere Him. John Piper says, "God is most glorified in us when we are most satisfied in him."[1] As I look back on my life, I wonder whether I've had a lifestyle of worship. Often, if I am brave enough to admit it, I've been less satisfied in God and more preoccupied with stress. Worship will be our primary occupation in heaven, but I often fail to ready myself for that upcoming task. And yet God desires our worship for His sake and for ours. He knows that as we elevate Him, our worries melt away. As we dare to let go of the idols we often worship (fame, money, beauty, sex, and power to name a few) and instead elevate His name in front of others, we will be blessed.

Our children will worship as we worship. As we center our lives around reverencing God, our children will too. To worship God is a profoundly countercultural task because it deals a decisive blow to our selfishness.

The Great Commandment

Jesus' command to us all was to love God—which often involves service and worship—and love others. We may get the "worship God" thing down, but that matters very little if we can't seem to become grateful for the people God has placed around us. In our families, we often fail to treat each other with kindness and gratefulness. I once was asked what the essence of our parenting was. It's this: Teach your children to respect each family member. We do not tolerate unkindness. We cherish and encourage thankfulness for every family member's uniqueness. Of course we fail. Of course we say things we shouldn't. Of course my children demonstrate ungratefulness toward each other. But we won't tolerate these things. Appearing holy and grateful might be easy; being thankful for your spouse, your children, and your extended family on a regular basis is another thing altogether.

Endure Through Entreating

Life is not merely about holding out, but about crying out. It's not sheer endurance, but entreating the one who brings joy. In one of our prayer letters I wrote these words: "Oh, that Jesus would shine in every last one of us, that people could see Jesus and not us as we endure. I pray for my children, that they'd sense the presence of Jesus Christ as they navigate their worlds, that they'd know His delight, His power, His strength, His life. May we be able to walk in faith, believing God is big enough to battle on our behalf." Life is never easy. Battles and strife often mark our paths. But we can always cry out to God, begging Him to help us, to lift our heads and to give us thankful hearts.

See Thankfulness as an Indicator

Thankfulness, or the lack of it, is perhaps the primary measuring stick of our closeness with Jesus. If we can train our children to understand that, we have given them a good gift. If our GQ (gratitude quotient) is low, something is wrong with the way we are relating to Jesus. Thankfulness and gratitude are peppered throughout the Bible:

- "Give thanks to the LORD, for he is good; his love endures forever" (1 Chronicles 16:34).

- "Let them give thanks to the LORD for his unfailing love and his wonderful deeds for men" (Psalm 107:21).

- "Devote yourselves to prayer, being watchful and thankful" (Colossians 4:2).

- "Always [give] thanks to God the Father for everything, in the name of the Lord Jesus Christ" (Ephesians 5:20).

- "Give thanks in all circumstances, for this is God's will for you in Christ Jesus" (1 Thessalonians 5:18).

When our family starts whining and complaining, we try to redirect our children to give thanks—not in a forced, inauthentic way, but invitationally. We ask, "Can you share one thing you're thankful for today?" The children usually come up with something immediately, and the mood of our home changes in an instant. And they are quick to remind me to count my blessings when I'm whining and complaining!

It's All from God

Everything we have is God's. He created everything we see, feel, touch, smell, and hear. With mystical adeptness, He created this world for us to enjoy. He created families. Everything we receive comes from His hand. The apostle Paul made this clear when he wrote, "For who makes you different from anyone else? What do you have that you did not receive? And if you did receive it, why do you boast as though you did not?" (1 Corinthians 4:7). We are like little children with open hands, and God pours blessings into them, spilling over our fingers and into our lives. My friend Jeanne understands this:

> We believe man's primary purpose is to glorify God and enjoy Him forever. We also acknowledge that everything we have is a gift—even down to the air we breathe and our ability to breathe it. If we succeed, we thank Him for the open door and the power to walk through it. If we stumble, we thank Him for picking us up again. We rejoice in knowing that God is able to do exceeding abundantly beyond all we ask or think, so that even if we screw up again and again, He is big enough to bring His purposes to pass. We ask Him to do this. We clothe ourselves in the phrases of the Lord's prayer and the armor of God, and we

simply believe He will accomplish His will, because He is God and no one can stay His hand. He is faithful. And, as though that weren't enough, He gives and perfects our faith. The real question is, how can we not worship and give thanks?[2]

The Opposite of Thankfulness: Pride

Gratitude has an enemy: self-centered pride. We can be too thankful for ourselves and our own piety and miss connecting deeply with Jesus. Remember the Pharisee who thanked God he was not like other sinners?[3] He missed Jesus because he was too preoccupied with his piety. Pharisees have a hard time being grateful folk.

And yet, in our evangelical culture, we seem to be parenting Pharisees. So much pressure exists for parents to produce perfect children that we unwittingly pressure our children to follow harder after rules than after Jesus. This neuters relationship. It kills thankfulness, shoving it to the far back of a child's mind. If he is so consumed with always acting correctly and having the correct answers, he will forget to be grateful for the little blessings God sends his way.

Ours is a gospel of grace, not works. And since it is all about the astounding grace Jesus demonstrated on the cross, we miss the mark if we emphasize piety over gratitude. Everything we have is a gift. Our relationship with Jesus is a gift. Our own ability to follow Him is a gift. Every good thing inside us is from Him. James says, "Every good and perfect gift is from above, coming down from the Father of the heavenly lights, who does not change like shifting shadows" (James 1:17). If we think that we can impress the Almighty with our stunning good works and our perfectly spoken theologies, we are sorely wrong.

The best place in Scripture this principle is demonstrated is Luke 15:11-32, where Jesus tells the Pharisees a story about two sons—one a prodigal and one a "good son." The hero of the story is the father, who waits in breathless anticipation for his wayward son to return home. The prodigal, after coming to his senses amid the pig slop, feels unworthy to return home, and yet he does. The father blesses him with a feast. I have no doubt the prodigal lived a life of gratitude from that moment on because the father lavished so much love on him. He had been forgiven much.

The "good son" who obeyed all the rules, perhaps begrudgingly, missed the point entirely. Instead of rejoicing that his brother has returned, he grumbled a self-centered whine.

> The older brother became angry and refused to go in. So his father went out and pleaded with him. But he answered his father, "Look! All these years I've been slaving for you and never disobeyed your orders. Yet you never gave me even a young goat so I could celebrate with my friends. But when this son of yours who has squandered your property with prostitutes comes home, you kill the fattened calf for him!" (Luke 15:28-30).

In his self-righteousness, the prodigal's brother forgot gratitude.

Yet his father reminded him of something important: Everything the father had was his in the first place. "'My son,' the father said, 'you are always with me, and everything I have is yours. But we had to celebrate and be glad, because this brother of yours was dead and is alive again; he was lost and is found'" (Luke 15:31). The crux of the matter is that God is always with us. We always have cause to rejoice. Gratitude should seep through our pores because God is always with us; everything He offers is ours.

I don't want to raise the prodigal's brother in my home. Sure, he may look good. He may feign obedience. But he misunderstands the goodness of God. Would you rather have a living, breathing child who occasionally doubts and sometimes stumbles, or a robot? Our task as parents is not to produce happy little robots who react mechanically to life and spit out appropriate words at appropriate times. Nor is it to shelter them in such a way that they feel life owes them something. This life Jesus calls us all to—parents and children alike—is a life of sacrifice and dependence. In that weakened, needy state, we become thankful. Joyful. Hopeful. We know that life is not all about us or our needs. It's about making Jesus smile from heaven. It's about His kingdom. It's about offering our lives in gratitude to a holy God.

⌒⊘⌒

Gracious followers of Jesus will entice the world. Self-serving, prideful Pharisees merely shake their finger and push others away.

What kind of faith do we want our children to bring to this postmodern world? A stoic, stuffy religion that beckons people to rules and regulations? Or a vibrant, life-giving, grace-abounding relationship with Jesus that infects and affects the people around them? What will attract a shifting culture to Jesus? It will be our invigorated, grateful hearts—authentic, broken hearts that dare to thank God in the midst of life's mess. That's what this world hungers for: a unique expression of the reality of Jesus played out on the field of postmodernity. As we dare to love and challenge our children in this world, teaching them to follow the path of the scarred Carpenter, we will begin to see how Jesus can infuse culture through them. They are missionaries, sent out to a culture we may not understand. To prepare them is our duty and joy.

Seventeen

The Story

Jacob glanced around his empty room. Posters ripped from the walls, bits of them remaining under still-shiny tacks. A hollow dresser, devoid of jeans and socks. A clean spot on his desk, dust all around, where his monitor once rested. He hoisted his suitcase through the door as boxes stacked high in the minivan beckoned him outside. Time to leave.

He remembered late nights with his parents and friends, sitting around the dinner table under the watchful gaze of candlelight, debating the validity of war, the stench of poverty. He loved that his friends, some who believed, others who searched, thought his parents approachable, real. He stopped in the kitchen and dropped his bag. There, haloed under fluorescent lights, his mother stood. A single tear inched down her cheek.

"I've learned so much from you," she told Jacob in a voice that sounded pinched.

Jacob hugged her, lifting her off her feet until she laughed—the laugh that taught him to be thankful for every little thing. "Thanks, Mom," was all he could muster. It didn't seem enough.

"It won't be the same here without you."

Jacob swallowed. "And I won't be the same without you."

Jacob's dad lumbered into the kitchen. He grabbed the suitcase. "Time to go," he said.

Jacob followed his father. He remembered following him around as a little kid, clinging to his leg as he left for work. He vowed then to never let his dad go. And now *he* was the one leaving. The one making his way in this crazy world.

Jacob watched as his father hefted his suitcase into the minivan. They'd had that van for years upon years. Dad never did want to sell it, he said. Too many memories of fishing trips and drives to the cabin. Though the engine turned over 100,000 three times and the body had survived two crashes, Jacob felt it was beautiful—the most beautiful van on earth.

Sitting on the porch swing while a lazy Seattle breeze teased his hair, Jacob thought of the future. College. Maybe working in a developing nation. Marriage. Kids. Snatches of his mother's life flashed before him—her gentle ways, her willing readiness to admit her faults to her children, the way she beautified their home with thrift. He thanked God for his father, who wrestled with the Bible as if it were a greased pig yet believed in its message of grace and love with fierce tenacity. He knew his father's shoulders were always big enough to handle Jacob's doubts, his questions.

They'd been surrounded by folks who felt the same way—whose authentic faith spilled out into helping others, living gently with the land, learning to offer grace and love to the unlovely. In this community Jacob learned to stand on his own two feet spiritually. This community cheered for him when he bungled worship for the first time on his guitar. This community loved him despite his tattoos and piercings. They loved the anger out of him.

His sister, Ellie, sat down beside him now, her small hand resting on his knee. He covered her hand with his.

"Jacob, don't go," Ellie said.

"I have to, Els. It's time."

"I don't want you to."

"I know."

They sat there swinging while Dad repacked the van again, readying it for the new adventure—this time where books and co-eds would populate Jacob's life.

"You promise to text me?"

Jacob ruffled Ellie's hair. "Of course. You know I will."

"What am I going to do if I try to text you and you're off running around campus?"

"Leave me a message. I'll make time for you." Jacob stood. "Don't be paranoid. I'm still your brother."

She laughed then. A laugh that sent a shiver through Jacob. He had wondered if she'd laugh again after cancer shot through her like an angry cannon. But she did. God, in His mercy, chose to heal Ellie while she laughed her way through with a strange sense of gratitude he only hoped he could emulate. Ellie's brush with heaven's gates started all the questioning. Her steadfast thankfulness brought him back to Jesus. There had to be more to life than making money and having toys. Ellie taught him that, not by her words but by her heart— her sweet, enduring heart.

Jacob hugged her tight, squeezing the breath from her. "I'll miss you," he choked.

"Dinner won't be the same," she breathed.

Jacob noticed Dad had started the van. It rumbled to life. He jumped in, slamming the door on the life he once had and wondered what life would hold for him.

"Let's go," his father said.

"I'm ready," Jacob said. *By God's grace.*

Notes

Chapter 2—A Need

1. Ivy Beckwith, *Postmodern Children's Ministry* (El Cajon, CA: Youth Specialties Books, 2004), pp. 16-17.

2. Brian McLaren, *The Church on the Other Side* (Grand Rapids: Zondervan, 2000), p. 177.

3. Dan Allender, *How Children Raise Parents* (Colorado Springs: WaterBrook Press, 2003), p. 4.

4. Mary Pipher, *The Shelter of Each Other* (New York: Ballantine Books, 1996), pp. 93-94.

Chapter 3—A Paradigm

1. Mark Driscoll, *The Radical Reformission* (Grand Rapids: Zondervan, 2004), p. 169.

2. See Don Richardson, *Eternity in Their Hearts* (Ventura: Regal Books, 1984).

3. Oswald Chambers, *My Utmost for His Highest* (Westwood, NJ: Barbour and Company, Inc., 1935), p. 6.

4. Renee Mills, Prayer E-mail Newsletter, January 9, 2006, used by permission.

5. Ibid.

Chapter 4—A New Tradition

1. Oswald Chambers, *My Utmost for His Highest* (Westwood, NJ, Barbour and Company, Inc., 1935), p. 11.

2. See Matthew 14:28-33.

3. Melanie Morales, e-mail dated January 3, 2006. Used by permission.

4. Mark Driscoll, *The Radical Reformission* (Grand Rapids: Zondervan, 2004), p. 35.

Chapter 5—The Truth

1. See John 18:38.

2. Jeanne Damoff, written interview, March 27, 2006.

3. Leslie Wilson, written interview, February 1, 2006.

Chapter 6—A Conversation

Epigraph. Marjorie Thompson, *Family: The Forming Center* (Nashville: Upper Room Books, 1996), p. 25.

1. Erin Teske, written interview, February 6, 2006.

2. Lisa Borden, written interview, February 15, 2006.

3. See Ephesians 6:4.

4. Renee Mills, written interview, January 10, 2006.

5. Brandy Prince, live interview, February 6, 2006.

6. Borden.

7. See Gary Smalley and Ross Campbell, *The Five Love Languages of Children* (Chicago: Moody Publishers, 1997).

8. Borden.

9. George and Jeanne Damoff, written interview, March 27, 2006.

Chapter 7—A Window

Epigraph. Dan Allender, *How Children Raise Parents* (Colorado Springs: WaterBrook Press, 2003), p. 6.

1. Ibid., p. 178.

2. Mary DeMuth, *Building the Christian Family You Never Had* (Colorado Springs: WaterBrook Press, 2006). See chapter 9 for more details.

Chapter 8—A Haven

1. Marjorie Thompson, *Family: The Forming Center* (Nashville: Upper Room Books, 1996), p. 57.

2. Ross Campbell, *How to Really Love Your Child* (Colorado Springs: Chariot Victor Publishing, 1992), p. 57.

3. George and Jeanne Damoff, written interview, February 15, 2006.

4. Lisa Borden, written interview, February 15, 2006.

5. Gladys Hunt, *Honey for a Child's Heart* (Grand Rapids: Zondervan Publishing House, 1989), p. 75.

6. Ibid., p. 77.

7. Ibid., p. 86.

8. See Brother Lawrence, *The Practice of the Presence of God* (New Kensington, PA: Whitaker House, 1982).

9. Esther de Waal, "The Extraordinary in the Ordinary," *Weavings* (May-June 1987), p. 15.

Chapter 9—A Masterpiece

1. Erin Teske, written interview, February 6, 2006.

2. Ken Gire, *Windows of the Soul* (Grand Rapids: Zondervan, 1996), p. 17.

3. For more information, visit www.24-7prayer.com.

4. Lisa Borden, written interview, February 15, 2006.

Chapter 10—A Coach

1. See www.loveandlogic.com.

2. See 1 Corinthians 13:4-7.

3. See Ken McDuff, "What's Wrong with 'Growing Kids God's Way'?" *Group Magazine*, July-August 1997, Volume 23, Number 5, pp. 39-42.

4. Jeanne Damoff, written interview, March 27, 2006.

5. Harper Lee, *To Kill a Mockingbird* (New York: Warner Books), p. 282.

Chapter 11—A Full Glass

1. A.W. Tozer, *The Pursuit of God* (Camp Hill, PA: Christian Publications Inc., 1983), p. 3.

Chapter 12—An Authenticity

Epigraph. Mary DeMuth, *Watching the Tree Limbs* (Colorado Springs: NavPress, 2006), p. 24.

1. Marjorie Thompson, *Family: The Forming Center* (Nashville: Upper Room Books, 1996), p. 41.

2. Tim Kimmel, *Grace-Based Parenting* (Nashville: W Publishing Group, 2004), p. 7.

3. See Nancy Leigh DeMoss, "The Beauty of Brokenness," *Real Family Life Magazine*, November 1997, pp. 10-11.

4. Lisa Samson, written interview, February 2006.

5. Henri Nouwen, *Mornings with Henri J.M. Nouwen* (Cincinnati: Charis Books, 1997), n.p.

6. Thompson, p. 41.

Chapter 13—The Bible

Epigraph. Ivy Beckwith, *Postmodern Children's Ministry* (Grand Rapids: Zondervan, 2004), p. 126.

1. Ibid., p. 125.

2. Rob Bell, *Velvet Elvis* (Grand Rapids: Zondervan, 2005), p. 62.

3. Gretchen Wolff Pritchard, *Offering the Gospel to Children* (Cambridge, MA: Cowley Publications, 1992), p. 14.

4. For more information, please see www.godlyplay.com.

5. Anne Lamott, *Plan B* (New York: Riverhead Books, 2005), p. 65.

6. Job 38:4,8,12,17,31,36.

Chapter 14—A Community

1. For a more thorough discussion of navigating difficult relatives, see chapter 15, "Why

Can't I Go to Grandpa's House?" in my book *Building the Christian Family You Never Had* (Colorado Springs: WaterBrook Press, 2006), pp. 141-148.

2. See www.30hourfamine.org for more information.

Chapter 15—A Kingdom

1. Dietrich Bonhoeffer, *The Cost of Discipleship* (New York: Collier Books, 1963), p. 7.

2. See Matthew 25:31-46.

3. Lisa Samson, blog dated April 30, 2006.

4. Justin Powell, e-mail dated April 10, 2006.

5. Jeanne Damoff, written interview, March 27, 2006.

6. Tim Kimmel, *Grace-Based Parenting* (Nashville: W Publishing Group, 2004), p. 11.

7. See Matthew 5:40-42.

8. Damoff.

Chapter 16—A Gift

1. John Piper, *Desiring God: Meditations of a Christian Hedonist* (Sisters, OR: Multnomah Publishers, 1996), p. 50.

2. Jeanne Damoff, written interview, March 27, 2006.

3. See Luke 18:11-13.

Questions for Group Discussion

Chapter 1—A Story

1. How does Jacob's story ring true today?

2. How can parents, in your opinion, better prepare their children for a postmodern world?

Chapter 2—A Need

1. Why is it important to understand the culture we live in?

2. In what ways does rethinking how we present Jesus to our culture deepen our relationship with Him?

3. How important is relevancy in presenting the gospel?

4. How have you found a balance between intellectually pursuing Jesus and experiencing His presence? How do your children interact with Jesus?

5. How have you or your children become lifelong learners?

Chapter 3—A Paradigm

1. After reading through the section about modernity, what in the modern perspective has enhanced the church? What has hindered it?

2. As our culture shifts, what aspects of postmodernity do you see as detrimental to the church? What aspects are beneficial?

3. Why is it important to contextualize the gospel, to find postmodern "redemptive analogies"?

4. How have Christians cocooned children from the world? How has that affected children?

5. Other than completely separating from the world, how can we as parents help our children remain unstained by the world and yet still engaged?

6. How have you cultivated your heart? How have you actively nurtured your child's heart?

Chapter 4—A New Tradition

1. In what ways have you parented your children out of fear or worry?

2. How can the story of Peter walking on water be a good metaphor for parenting in today's postmodern world?

3. What does "parenting by braille" look like in your home? What appeals to you about parenting this way? What bothers you?

Chapter 5—The Truth

1. Can we know absolute truth?

2. How do people from a modern perspective miss truth? How do postmoderns miss it? In what ways?

3. Choose one of the Proverbs mentioned in this chapter and discuss it as a group. How is it helpful to you as you parent in a postmodern world?

4. Why is Jacob's story in this chapter important to remember?

Chapter 6—A Conversation

1. How have you parented around the dinner table?

2. What is *peripatetic* spirituality, and how have you seen it in operation in your family? Give examples.

3. How have your children been encouraging to you in the past week? How have you chosen to verbally encourage each child?

4. Is it difficult for you to ask your children for forgiveness? Why or why not?

5. How have you created a safe environment for your children to share their hearts?

6. Why should parenting be purposeful?

7. How have you created space and time for your children in this crazy-busy life?

8. Grace and truth are difficult to balance. Give an example of when you've leaned more toward grace, sacrificing truth. When have you shared the truth without grace? How did you feel both times?

Chapter 7—A Window

1. In the past month, how have you heard the voice of Jesus in your children? What did you learn?

2. How have your children helped you slow down?

3. What is your fondest memory of playing with or alongside your children? How did that connect you to Jesus?

4. In what ways has parenting helped you understand God's affection for you?

Chapter 8—A Haven

1. How has your home been like a haven? When has it *not* been a haven? Why?

2. In your group, brainstorm ways parents can show kindness to children. Choose one way you'd like to show kindness this week.

3. What hard questions have your children asked you?

4. How have you learned to be present with your children?

5. In what ways have you dealt with media in your home? Would you like to change the amount of media your children see?

6. Share a story when you spent time outdoors with your children. How did it go? How did you connect?

7. What books have been the most influential as you've read to your children? Why?

8. What role does humor play in your parenting? Would your children say you are able to laugh at life's barbs? Why or why not?

Chapter 9—A Masterpiece

1. How have your children's masterpieces shown you what's inside them?

2. In what ways have you interacted with your children through doing art together?

3. Do you tell childhood stories? Why or why not?

4. How has music bound you together? How has it separated you?

Chapter 10—A Coach

1. How have you prevented pain in your child's life?

2. What is the best question you've asked in the last week?

3. Read Proverbs 22:6. Discuss which directions your children are taking. How did God create them? What makes each one tick?

4. When have you jumped on "the lecture circuit," and how did that affect your children?

Chapter 11—A Full Glass

1. How have you settled for "turbulence of the soul"?

2. In what ways are you weary and heavy burdened as a parent? As a spouse? As a church member? As a worker?

3. Over the past year, would you use the word *abundance* to define your life? The lives of your children?

4. Would a good friend describe you as resilient? Why or why not?

Chapter 12—An Authenticity

1. Who is the most authentic person you know? Why do you think he or she is authentic? How is he or she able to be that way?

2. How does sharing our weakness endear us to our children? Is sharing your weakness difficult for you? Why or why not?

3. Should we tell our children everything? Why or why not?

4. How does brokenness relate to authenticity and following Jesus? How does brokenness help us to parent differently?

5. Give an example of how speaking the truth in love has brought healing to your family.

Chapter 13—The Bible

1. Why is the Bible not merely an instruction manual?

2. How have you wrestled with the difficult passages of the Bible?

3. In what ways have you reduced God's Word, if you have, to that which is manageable?

4. Why does realizing our brain's capacity help us deal with the Bible's difficulty?

5. What are the essentials of the Christian faith? What tenets or beliefs would you die for? What are some peripheral issues?

Chapter 14—A Community

1. The author wrote, "Community is what shapes our souls." How is that true? How have you seen this happen in your own life?

2. Should we welcome all rapscallions into our homes? Why or why not?

3. When have you seen your children revel in the beauty of people?

4. What if no church programs were available to you? What would you do if the responsibility of creating community in your home was yours? Who would you bring into your circle? Why?

5. How has your church provided community?

Chapter 15—A Kingdom

1. If you asked your children what "take up your cross" meant, what would each say?

2. In what ways have you encouraged your children to follow the radical call of Jesus?

3. Describe the last time you served less-privileged people together as a family. What happened? How did your children respond?

4. Over the past six months, how have you encountered spiritual warfare as a family? How did your family grow?

Chapter 16—A Gift

1. Read Psalm 3:3. How has God lifted your head this week? Describe a time when He lifted the head of one of your children.

2. What does it look like to have an eternal perspective permeate our homes?

3. What ways do you enjoy worshipping God as a family?

4. With your group, thank God for each family member. Be specific.

Chapter 17—The Story

1. How does Jacob's new story encourage you?

2. With your group, describe one of your children's last days at home. What would you want them to remember? How would you like to launch them? And what would you love them to say about you and how you parented?

Helpful Resources

Books dealing with postmodernity and Christianity:

Beckwith, Ivy. *Postmodern Children's Ministry* (El Cajon, CA: Youth Specialties Books, 2004).

Bell, Rob. *Velvet Elvis: Repainting the Christian Faith* (Grand Rapids: Zondervan, 2005).

Driscoll, Mark. *The Radical Reformission* (Grand Rapids: Zondervan, 2004).

McLaren, Brian D. *The Church on the Other Side* (Grand Rapids: Zondervan, 2000).

Miller, Donald. *Blue like Jazz: Nonreligious Thoughts on Christian Spirituality* (Nashville: Nelson Books, 2003).

Myers, Joseph. *The Search to Belong: Rethinking Intimacy, Community and Small Groups* (Grand Rapids: Zondervan, 2003).

Winner, Lauren. *Girl Meets God: A Memoir* (New York: Random House Trade Paperbacks, 2003).

Parenting books:

Allender, Dan. *How Children Raise Parents* (Colorado Springs: WaterBrook Press, 2003).

Cline, Foster, and Jim Fay. *Parenting with Love and Logic* (Colorado Springs: Pinon Press, 1990).

Kimmel, Tim. *Grace-Based Parenting* (Nashville: W Publishing Group, 2004).

Miller-McLemore, Bonnie J. *Let the Children Come* (San Francisco: Jossey-Bass, 2003).

Pipher, Mary. *The Shelter of Each Other* (New York: Ballantine Books, 1996).

If you wish to connect with Mary,
she invites you to contact her at

mary@marydemuth.com
or **www.marydemuth.com**

To learn more about Harvest House books
or to read sample chapters, log on to our website:
www.harvesthousepublishers.com

HARVEST HOUSE PUBLISHERS

EUGENE, OREGON